Language & Writing 7

David Hodgkinson

Nelson Language & Writing Authors

Don Aker
David Hodgkinson
Michael Kamann, Senior Author

I(T)P Nelson

Variety! Each of the 16 units focuses on a different form of writing.

This feature previews the language skills you'll be learning.

A brief introduction helps you get your bearings....

Unit 6 Comparison

At the end of this unit you will

Know
- the characteristics of a comparison
- the rules for forming comparatives and superlatives
- letters and patterns that make the sound of **k**

Be Able To
- write a comparison
- identify the subject and direct and indirect in a sentence
- use apostrophes c

What is a comparison?

Comparison is a powerful writing technique used in English, science, geography, and many other subjects. By identifying the common features of two or more persons, places, actions, or things, and then describing how these features differ, a comparison allows the reader to understand a topic more clearly. In the following article, Mike Fabbro compares skiing to snowboarding.

I never fully appreciated the popularity of snowboarding with kids until I saw two young boys—one a skier, the other a snowboarder—walking through the village at Mont Tremblant. The skier looked frustrated as he trudged along in his huge ski boots, buckles undone for flexibility, occasionally sliding on ice. In his one-piece, Barney-purple ski suit, he clutched his skis and poles in a desperate attempt not to drop them. He just didn't look like a happy little camper.

The snowboarder, on the other hand, was hip—and he knew it. He was darting back and forth in his snowboard boots like he was wearing runners; comfort and traction weren't a concern. He carried all of the necessary equipment—his board with ease under one arm as he waved and boasted of the day's adventures. He wore a small backpack that probably contained his lunch—and cell phone.

62

It's a myth that snow than skiing for any particular support it. However, there are prior to snowboarding. The si traversing are all quite simila easily transferred. There are safety and on-hill etiquette. to deal with flats and steeps and it's easier to do that on on and off lifts on skis, and than snowboarding when fi

Almost every ski snowboard the s ograms for sn b lalized, in the sam is are. Look for a sn n a proven program. S ould always be a fun e especially learning how.

4. Write your paragraph, informatio complete y

5. Refer back satisfied w photos or your grou feedback.

 Tech
It's of word with

GRA

The simp or what

The sim words)

The most predicate the simp

Joh

However meaning *backpac* sentence in this

A di actio

Leading off each unit—some writing to grab your attention. All the language instruction in the unit builds on the opening model.

You'll find plenty of tips, strategies, ideas, and challenges in these special boxes.

For your convenience, we've highlighted the most important definitions and rules.

Welcome
to Nelson Language & Writing

Welcome to *Nelson Language & Writing*, specially designed to boost your language skills and improve your writing. Here is what you will find inside...

When you see this logo, reach for your favourite pen! The best way to learn new language skills is to apply them in your own writing.

Each unit teaches Grammar, Mechanics, Usage & Style, and Spelling skills, and includes a Writer's Workshop to guide you step by step through the writing process.

You can see the goal(s) of each lesson at a glance.

The spelling lists (which you can customize) can help you increase your vocabulary and strengthen your spelling.

We've included a wide variety of activities that allow you to practise new skills.

...sing information from A in your first ...rom B in your second paragraph, and ...e concluding paragraph. You should ...th a concluding comment.

...point and revise your writing until you are ...content, and organization. If possible, bring in ...e things you are comparing to show members of ...your comparison with your group for their

...accompany comparisons with charts or tables. Many ...grams allow you to make pie charts and graphs ...mouse. Check out your program for details.

Language Link

Be Able To
- identify the subject, predicate, and direct and indirect object in a sentence

...f a sentence is the noun or pronoun that tells who ...is about.

...e of a sentence is the main verb (one or more ...t the subject is or does.

...ces are made up of a simple subject and a simple ...wing sentences, the simple subject is in bold, and ...s in italics.

Skates *glide.*   **Children** *play.*

...s require more than just a subject to complete their ...e, in the sentence *He wore a backpack*, the word ...the meaning of the sentence. Without it, the rest of the ...make sense. Words that complete the meaning of a verb ...d **objects.**

...is a noun or pronoun that receives the action of an ...ct objects answer the questions *what* or *who.*

Unit **6** Comparison

65

Language Link

SPELLING

In words where you hear a **k** sound, chances are the sound is made by the letter **k** or patterns such as **nk**, **lk**, or **ke**. In some cases, however, the sound can be made by **c**, **ck**, or **qu**.

Words to Watch For

These words, taken from the comparison at the beginning of the unit, all have a **k** sound.

buckle   backpack   etiquette   athletic   dynamic
traction   statistics   gymnastics   physical   unique

In your notebook, make a list of 8-10 words that make the sound of **k**. You can use words from this box, the comparison piece, and your personal reading. To help you learn the words, underline letters or patterns that make the sound of **k**.

1. Fill in the missing letters to complete **Words to Watch For**. Write them in your notebook.
   a) _ t _ _ _ _ _ e   b) _ _ n _ _ i _   c) _ _ _ c _ _ _ _   d) _ _ a _ _ _ _ _ _

2. Use the **Words to Watch For** to complete these sentences. Write the words in your notebook.
   a) Broken legs are sometimes put in _____.
   b) _____ show that you are much safer when you use safety gear.
   c) It's important to learn on-hill _____.

3. **Words to Watch For** includes two pairs of words whose last syllables rhyme. What are they? Using words from your list and other words with the **k** sound, create at least four other rhyming pairs. Use these words to create a poem that rhymes. Read your poem aloud to a group or the class.

Scroll Back

Edit and proofread your comparison, paying particular attention to the following:
- ☐ Have you used apostrophes correctly?
- ☐ Have you used the correct comparative or superlative form of any modifiers?
- ☐ Have you spelled all words correctly, especially those with the **k** sound?

Know
- letters and patterns that make the sound of **k**

Unit **6** Comparison

69

International Thomson Publishing

© Copyright 1998 by ITP® Nelson

www.thomson.com

ISBN 0-17-606570-9

Cataloguing in Publication Data

Hodgkinson, Dave
        Nelson language and writing 7

ISBN 0-17-606570-9

1. English language - Grammar - Juvenile literature. 2. English language - Composition and exercises - Juvenile literature. I. Title.

PE1112.H63 1998   428.2   C97-931911-0

Team Leader/Publisher:	Mark Cobham
Acquisitions Editor:	Tara Steele
Project Editors:	David Friend and Jennifer Rowsell
Series Editors:	Chelsea Donaldson, Joanne Close, Karen Alliston
Art Direction:	Ken Phipps
Cover Designer:	Ken Phipps
Senior Designers:	Brian Cartwright, Daryn Dewalt, Peggy Rhodes, Todd Ryoji
Senior Composition Analyst:	Daryn Dewalt
Production Coordinator:	Theresa Thomas
Permissions:	Vicki Gould
Film:	Quadratone Graphics Ltd.

Printed and bound in Canada
2 3 4 5   02 01 00 99 98

Acknowledgments

Permission to reprint copyright material is gratefully acknowledged. Every reasonable effort to trace the copyright holders of materials appearing in this book has been made. Information that will enable the publisher to rectify any error or omission will be welcome.

"Father's Day" by permission of Joseph Mitchell. "A Million Dollars" from 2500 ANECDOTES FOR ALL OCCASIONS by Edmund Fuller (ed.). Copyright © 1952, 1980 by Crown Publishers, Inc. Reprinted by permission of Crown Publishers. Steve Tambellini anecdote © 1991 Stan Fischler. "The Camel and the Mouse" and by Rumi and "The Oh So Grand Ox, and the Poor Pathetic Frog" by LaFontaine reprinted by permission of Philomel Books from FEATHERS AND TAILS: ANIMAL TALES retold by David Kherdian, text copyright © 1992 by David Kherdian. "The Wolf and the Lamb" from AESOP AND COMPANY. Text copyright © 1991 by Barbara Bader. Reprinted by permission of Houghton Mifflin Company. All rights reserved. Excerpts from AESOP & COMPANY. Text copyright © 1991 by Barbara Bader. Reprinted by permission of Houghton Mifflin Company. All rights reserved. *Little by Little* by Jean Little. Copyright © Jean Little, 1987. Reprinted by permission of Penguin Books Canada Limited. *The Root Cellar* by Janet Lunn from Canadian Children's Treasury © 1988 by Key Porter Books. "You, Your Kids and Snowboarding" by Mike Fabbro from "Ski Canada Buyers Guide '98." Reprinted with permission. "Surf City, CDA" © 1997 Brian Payton, from *Long Beach, Clayoquot and Beyond* (Raincoast Books). "The Shark" by E. J. Pratt from E.J. PRATT: COMPLETE POEMS, VOL. 1 AND 2 edited by Djwa & Moyles. Reprinted by permission of University of Toronto Press Incorporated. "The Flying Bomb" from *Great Mistakes*, Copyright © 1979 by Daniel Cohen. Reprinted by permission of the publisher, M. Evans and Company, Inc. "Picnicking Procedures" from Honda published in *Shape* magazine, June 1997. "Bubble Gum" reprinted from WHERE DOES THIS COME FROM, BUBBLE GUM © 1989 by H. I. Peeples. Used with permission by NTC/Contemporary Publishing Company, Chicago. "Why Mosquitoes Suck" by Patricia Gadsby from *Discover* magazine, August 1997. "The So-Called Teenage Problem" by Tristan Zimmerman, a 17-year-old who actively participates in the local music scene and enjoys the infrequent pleasures of skateboarding. He aspires to become a professional artist of sorts. "Triumph" motorcycle advertisement from Eastern Marketing, 1996. For more information or your nearest Triumph dealer, call 1 888 4 TRI CAN. "Great Canadian Scientists" from YES Mag: Canada's Science Magazine For Kids. Great Canadian Scientists image from Great Canadian Scientists by Barry Shell. Get the book or visit the Website: www.science.ca

Reviewers

The authors and publishers gratefully acknowledge the contributions of the following educators:

Carol Anastasi Mississauga, Ontario	Irene Heffel Edmonton, Alberta
David Bergen Winnipeg, Manitoba	Pat Lychak Edmonton, Alberta
Steve Britton Winnipeg, Manitoba	Sharon Morris Toronto, Ontario
Christopher Carroll Langley, British Columbia	Louis Quildon Hamilton, Ontario
Arlene Christie Calgary, Alberta	Sandra Roy Kitchener, Ontario
Dena Domijan Burnaby, British Columbia	Rick Smith Odessa, Ontario
Genevieve Dowson Hamilton, Ontario	Steven Van Zoost Windsor, Nova Scotia
Karen Gatto Kitchener, Ontario	

Contents

Contents

Language Strands
(Mini-Lessons by Category)

Language Strands

The Writing Process

You're probably familiar with the stages of the writing process: prewriting, drafting, revising, editing and proofreading, and presenting. You probably also know how *messy* the writing process can be. You might find yourself reorganizing your information as you write. Or you might be well into the revising stage when you suddenly realize that you have to go back and think again about your purpose in writing. That's why we've put in all the two-way arrows in the diagram (and why our little writer person spends a lot of time darting back and forth between stages).

In the first stage, **prewriting**, you choose a topic, define your purpose and audience, and organize your ideas. Notice the arrows that point to and away from this stage. Prewriting connects to all the other stages because the questions you ask yourself at the outset about audience and purpose really determine how you will write, revise, *and* edit your work.

So now you've transformed the whirling thoughts in your head into a structured list of the things you want to write about. If you're like our little writer person, you're excited: you've progressed to the **drafting** stage. As you write, you'll need to remember your purpose, your audience, and your plan of organization. Think about how to capture your audience's attention (and how to keep it)—but try not to worry much about what your writing sounds like, or about details of grammar, spelling, usage, or punctuation. This is the time to let it *flow!*

When you're **revising** your draft, you need to consider three things: focus, content, and organization. Have you done what you set out to do? Is your writing style geared to the people you want to reach? Is there anything that you've missed, that you want to expand on, move somewhere else, or cut altogether? Now is the time to decide. Be brave, be ruthless, listen to your inner voice—and make those changes! Then go make yourself some hot chocolate.

By the time you're ready for **editing and proofreading**, you should be more or less satisfied that you've achieved your purpose in writing. This stage is a time for tinkering with words, and for tidying up mistakes in grammar, spelling, usage, and puncutation. (The units in this book will give you lots of ideas about what to look for when you're editing.) Finally, when you're **presenting** your work, make sure that it looks sharp: that it's clearly laid out, and nicely bound together. In other words, give your presentation some polish!

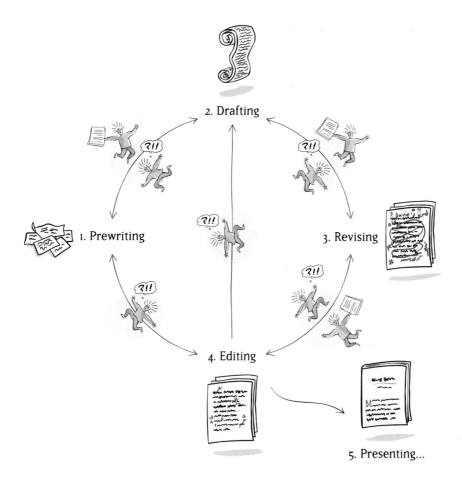

2. Drafting

1. Prewriting

3. Revising

4. Editing

5. Presenting...

Tony Gets an Assignment
(or, The Web and Flow of a Writer's Life)

Tony has been given a writing assignment:

> *Write a biographical incident that reveals something about the personality of someone you know.*

Tony is stumped. Blocked. In short, he can't think of a *thing*.

1. PREWRITING

No, we're not talking about going out and buying pens. This is the stage where you think about what you want to write about, and whether it will work as a topic. (For example, you might *want* to write a biographical incident that reveals the personality of Binky your goldfish, but this might not work if Binky doesn't *have* a personality.)

Tony figured that the best way to begin was to make a list of everyone he knew. Just looking at the list helped him to think of a few incidents, and here's the web he made of those events:

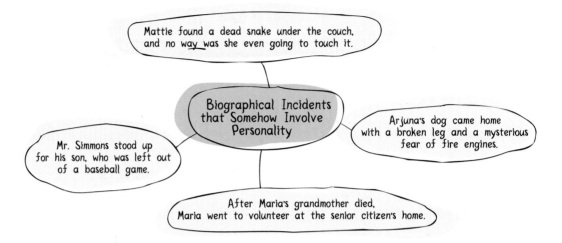

Mattie found a dead snake under the couch, and no way was she even going to touch it.

Biographical Incidents that Somehow Involve Personality

Arjuna's dog came home with a broken leg and a mysterious fear of fire engines.

Mr. Simmons stood up for his son, who was left out of a baseball game.

After Maria's grandmother died, Maria went to volunteer at the senior citizen's home.

Choosing a Topic

When **choosing a topic**, ask yourself

What do I find interesting about this topic?
Do I know enough about this topic to write about it?
Does this topic meet the assignment requirements?

Tony considered these four incidents, and finally decided to write about Mr. Simmons. What Mr. Simmons did had really impressed Tony. He remembered it well; it wouldn't take too much time to describe; and above all, it revealed a strength of character about Mr. Simmons that Tony hadn't seen before.

Defining a Purpose and Audience

When **defining your purpose and audience**, ask yourself

Why am I writing this?
Who am I writing for?

Your answers will affect everything, from what you say to how you say it, so it's worth doing a little thinking beforehand to save yourself time and effort later.

After asking the question "Why am I writing this?" Tony couldn't help himself: "I'm writing this because I have to!"

But Tony has chosen to tell this *particular* story because he has very clear memories of Mr. Simmons, who was Tony's grade two teacher. Because of an illness, Mr. Simmons had a patch over one eye and walked with a cane. Everyone thought he was a good teacher, but one day Tony was inspired by something that Mr. Simmons did outside of the classroom. And now Tony would like to capture that moment. His audience? Well, his teacher, obviously. And the other kids in the class (some of whom remember Mr. Simmons from elementary school).

Organizing Ideas

When **organizing ideas**, ask yourself

> Does the type of writing suggest a possible order?
> What order will make my ideas most interesting/understandable/appealing to my audience?
> What key words will help me order my ideas?

Tony has generated a list of details he wants to include. Because he's writing a narrative, he's decided that chronological order makes the most sense. Here's his outline:

- spring excitement
- baseball season
- Douglas Simmons wants to play baseball with the boys
- he's clumsy—lack of practice, so not as good as the other boys
- Mr. Simmons gives Douglas baseball glove hoping he'll be able to play with other kids
- watches as Douglas tries to join a ball game on playground
- Douglas feels rejected
- Mr. Simmons feels bad, both for son and for himself
- realizes his illness has affected more than just himself— his son too

2. DRAFTING

When **drafting**, ask yourself

> What's my purpose and who is my audience?
> How will I get and keep my audience's attention?
> What key words or phrases can I use to keep my writing logical and easy to follow?

The Writing Process

Outline in hand, Tony got out his lucky pen and set to work. Well, actually, he stared at the page for some time, pen poised to begin.

If you're finding it hard to get the words down, try

- setting a timer for ten minutes and writing nonstop about anything
- recopying what you've already written
- explaining to a friend or classmate what you're trying to say
- refocusing on your purpose and your audience

Tony knew he needed a great beginning: *On that fateful day, so long ago, the sun was shining, the birds were singing....* Oh man, this was harder than he thought.

To get your audience's attention, try

- starting with a question that will make them think
- using dialogue
- quoting an expert
- presenting an interesting fact

Tony finally began his draft with a description of Mr. Simmons looking out the school window at the boys playing baseball, the details of his illness, and how it had prevented him from playing baseball with his son. Tony strayed a bit from his outline because he realized that all this information was important for the point of the story.

But after a couple of pages Tony got worried because he hadn't even *started* writing about the actual incident. (And the whole thing was supposed to be only a few paragraphs!) So he crammed the rest of the story into one more paragraph. Tony, now hunched over his desk and writing furiously, ended with a fluorish: *"How is my son supposed to learn how to play if you don't let him?" cried the heartbroken Mr. Simmons to the boys, and tears were brimming in his one eye.*

There. Done! Tony leaned back in his chair, thinking his private thoughts. (They sounded something like this: "Yep, yep, yep. Am I good or *what?*")

3. REVISING

When **revising**, ask yourself

Are my purpose and audience clear?
What do I like best about my writing?
Does every part of the writing relate to my purpose?
Is there anything missing?

Revision can be the most difficult part of the writing process. We're so close to our own writing that it's hard to be objective about it. So, if possible, don't revise your work right away. Let it sit overnight or longer, so that you can gain some perspective on it. That's what Tony did. When he read his amazing creation a couple of days later—well, he wrinkled his brow. Narrowed his eyes. Pursed his lips. Hmm. Perhaps it needed a *little* work....

When you revise your draft, try to look at the big picture before you tackle the details. Concentrate on three things: focus, content, and organization.

Focus

Writing is focused if

- it's structured to emphasize the main point
- it achieves the purpose you set out to achieve
- it's directed at the audience you set out to write for

Content

When checking the content of your writing, make sure

- everything you say helps you to achieve your purpose
- you've included enough information for your audience
- you haven't included any unnecessary information

Organization

When revising the order of your writing, decide if

- the information is arranged to suit your purpose and audience
- any paragraphs or sentences should be added, deleted, or rearranged to make your point more effectively

When Tony really considered his draft he realized that he'd have to make some changes. He needed to shorten the introductory part about Mr. Simmons (too much description at the beginning sort of slowed things down, and maybe all the details about his illness weren't so important after all). He'd also need to make the incident itself more dramatic (shorter sentences, more dialogue), and end on a more positive note. Tony saw that his last sentence made Mr. Simmons sound kind of pathetic, and actually the *point* of the story was the exact *opposite.*

Sigh.

4. EDITING AND PROOFREADING

When **editing and proofreading**, ask yourself

Have I used as few words as possible to achieve my purpose?
Are my words well chosen, given my audience and purpose?
Are my sentences clear?
What particular grammar, mechanics, usage, and spelling errors should I check for?

At last Tony had a draft that he was happy with—or at least, that said what he wanted it to say. Now it was time to polish his writing.

But it can be difficult to edit your work if you don't know what to look for. The units in this book contain mini-lessons that will help you to focus on a few points in each piece of writing you do. That way, as you become aware of the mistakes you tend to make, you can gradually compile your own list of what to watch for when you edit.

- Look for ways to make your writing sound better (word choice, sentence variety, etc.).
- Correct grammatical, mechanical, and spelling errors (compile your own checklist of things to watch for).
- Say what you want to say using as few words as possible. Be ruthless.
- Keep a personal dictionary of words you frequently misspell.
- Get someone else to help you proofread your work.

Now, Tony happens to be a little weak in the spelling department, but fortunately he knows it. For help he turned to his friends Chris and Mattie. They found several spelling mistakes, and also discovered (annoyingly) that Tony has a tendency to write run-on sentences.

Here's the final draft of Tony's biographical incident.

The snow had melted and it was the time of year for baseball. Gerald Simmons had loved playing ball as a kid. Now, a cane and the patch over his left eye forced him to watch the students from the window of his classroom. That morning, he had given his son his old baseball glove, hoping that Douglas would enjoy the sport as much as he had.

Douglas gulped the last bite of his lunch and rushed out with his dad's old-fashioned glove. He stumbled out to the field, to find the teams already picked and the first pitches thrown. "What team am I on?" Douglas called enthusiastically. "What team do I play for?" he repeated the question uneasily. There was no response.

From his window, Mr. Simmons watched Douglas retreat, dangling the unused glove. Angrily, he reached for his cane and headed out to the baseball diamond. He ached as he remembered that he had never been able to practise with Douglas because of his health. "How is my son supposed to learn how to play if you don't let him?" he cried.

But he was a teacher as well as a father, and acceptance was a lesson he could help these children to learn. With a shrug, he regained his composure. "I haven't been able to help him," he said simply. "He needs a chance and I'm asking you to give it to him." And with that Mr. Simmons turned and walked slowly away.

Way to go, Tony! Look at his first paragraph: in just four sentences he sets the scene, introduces Mr. Simmons, and leads into Douglas's dilemma. Notice how his sentences flow, and how each paragraph has a central focus and moves the story forward. This helps to keep his readers interested. Tony has even used some vivid verbs that help the reader visualize the action. And Tony has organized his whole story around that one final character-revealing moment (which, as you'll recall, was the whole purpose of the piece).

Good writing seems effortless when you read it, but it can take a lot of thinking, rewriting, revising, and correcting before it reaches its final form. (Ask Tony.) The rest of this book can help you cultivate the skills you'll need to develop, shape, and polish your writing. Now get out your lucky pen.

Narration

Narration, the telling of a story, is as much a part of our culture as the food we eat or the clothing we wear. Although many people think of novels and short stories as the most common forms of narration, there are stories everywhere around us. Letters we write and receive, cafeteria chatter, and even our telephone conversations are filled with narratives, because when people share an experience with others, they often do so by telling a story.

This section contains four forms of narrative writing: anecdote, fable, autobiography, and friendly letter or e-mail. Although they vary in length and purpose, they all tell stories that catch and hold our interest.

Features of Narration

- A narrative is a story developed from an event or series of events.
- Character, setting, and mood are usually established at the beginning of the story.
- The middle describes events in which a character deals with some kind of conflict.
- The end of the story, or climax, tells how the conflict is resolved.

Unit ① Anecdote

What is an anecdote?

An anecdote is a short, entertaining account of an interesting or humorous incident. Anecdotes can stand by themselves, or can be a part of a longer story. Here are three anecdotes for you to read.

I

Given the assignment of writing a composition about what they would do if they had a million dollars, all of the students in the class except Justin were busily writing away.

The teacher, becoming aware that Justin was daydreaming, questioned him: "Justin, don't you know that you are supposed to tell what you would do if you had a million dollars?"

"Well," said the boy, lazily leaning back on his chair, "this is exactly what I would do if I had a million dollars."

II

Charles Chaplin Jr. liked to tell about the time his father attended a contest to see who could do the best Chaplin imitation. Dozens of contestants, all wearing the battered black hat and baggy suit and carrying the trademark cane, got up and did their best to simulate the famous walk and two or three of the movements that made Chaplin known throughout the world. Without identifying himself, Chaplin got up on the stage and did the routine. He came in third.

Know

- the characteristics of an anecdote
- the function of nouns
- the difference between common and proper nouns
- some of the letter patterns that represent the long vowel sounds

Be Able To

- write an anecdote
- use the proper punctuation and capitalization when writing dialogue
- use *accept* and *except* correctly

III

In August 1983, the New York Yankees were at Exhibition Stadium for a game against the Toronto Blue Jays. The Yankees had just finished their turn at bat in the fifth inning, and their outfielders were warming up by throwing a ball back and forth. With the Toronto batter about to get up, left-fielder Dave Winfield threw the ball in the direction of the Yankee bullpen.

The ball never reached its destination. A sea gull was calmly walking in front of the Yankee bullpen, and Winfield's throw hit the bird straight on....

Winfield was placed under arrest after the game and charged with "willfully causing unnecessary cruelty to animals." The charges were later dropped, of course, but not before the Toronto press had gotten a great deal of mileage out of a pretty insubstantial incident.

Not too surprisingly, Yankee manager Billy Martin had the last word about the affair. "They say Winfield hit the gull on purpose," Martin said. "They wouldn't say that if they could see the throws he's been making all year."

Idea File

Find other examples of anecdotes in books and magazines, or ask relatives to relate funny or interesting stories about members of your family.

21

Checkpoint: Anecdote

Look for these characteristics of an anecdote in the models. Later, you can use the list to help you revise your own work.

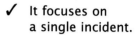

✓ It focuses on a single incident.

✓ It often includes dialogue.

✓ The climax usually comes in the last line(s), often in the form of a punch line.

✓ It is usually short (one to three paragraphs) and to the point.

1. Brainstorm a list of funny or interesting events that have happened to you or someone you know.

2. Decide which of your topics you want to write about. Then make a chart like the one shown below. You might start by writing the punch line under "End." Then fill in the necessary details under each heading.

Beginning	Middle	End

Idea File

Possible topics for a personal anecdote:

Something that happened in class or while playing a sport.

A funny story about something you did or said as a child.

A joke with a humorous punch line that you could write in your own words.

3. Now try writing a draft of your story. Keep it short, and make the punch line stand out.

4. Refer back to the Checkpoint and revise your anecdote until you are satisfied with its focus, content, and organization.

GRAMMAR

A **noun** is a word that names a person, place, thing, idea, or quality.

Know
- the function of nouns
- the difference between common and proper nouns

Aesop   Greece   anecdote   truth   beauty

1. Choose 10 nouns from the model anecdotes and write them in your notebook under the following headings: PEOPLE, ANIMALS, PLACES, THINGS, IDEAS, QUALITIES (or FEELINGS). Add other nouns to the chart until you have at least three nouns in each column.

2. Working with a partner, use nouns to build a staircase of 20 steps. Here is an example of the first steps:

```
stadium
      a
      n
      a
      g
      e
      routine
            f
            f
            e
            c
            t
```

Common nouns name persons, places, or things, but they are not capitalized, except at the beginning of a sentence. **Proper nouns** name specific persons, places, or things, and are always capitalized.

Common Noun	Proper Noun
cat	Garfield
trophy	Stanley Cup
girl	Linda
planet	Mars

3. The following is an anecdote told by hockey player Steve Tambellini. Using your notebook, copy all the nouns in the piece. Then circle any proper nouns.

> I played on the New York Islanders' first Stanley Cup-winning team ... and that was really something to behold, especially the celebrations we had after the championship was ours. The one party I remember above all was at [Islanders' left-winger] Clark Gillies's house.... Somebody managed to bring the Stanley Cup along in all its shining splendour. In the middle of the party, Gillies remembered he had to feed his dog, a huge German shepherd. He filled the top of the Stanley Cup with dog food and the next thing I knew I was viewing an unbelievable sight: a huge dog having dinner out of the Stanley Cup!

Strategy

In your writing, always try to use the most specific noun possible. Doing so will make your writing much more vivid. For example, *stadium* paints a clearer picture than *building*.

4. Write a single, specific noun that could replace each of the following expressions.

   a) a large stadium
   b) a one-storey house
   c) a fancy sports car
   d) a fast, busy road

MECHANICS

Be Able To
- use the proper punctuation and capitalization when writing dialogue

Dialogue is used frequently in narratives to give insight into a character or to advance the story. In anecdotes, the punch line is often written as a line of dialogue.

1. Use the examples given on the next page to help you complete each of the following rules about punctuating and capitalizing dialogue. The number of spaces indicates the number of words needed. Write each completed rule in your notebook.

a) Always enclose a character's direct speech _____ _____ _____ and begin the quotation with a _____ letter.

The teacher questioned him: "Justin, don't you know that you are supposed to tell what you would do if you had a million dollars?"

b) Do _____ use quotation marks with indirect speech.

The teacher asked Justin if he knew what he was supposed to be writing.

c) A character's direct speech is always separated from the rest of the sentence by a _____ or an end mark, which is always placed _____ the quotation marks.

"They say Winfield hit the gull on purpose," Martin said. "They wouldn't say that if they could see the throws he's been making all year!"

2. Compose a passage in which you break every rule above. Give your passage to a partner to correct the errors of punctuation and capitalization.

A Challenge

Collect interesting or humorous quotations from famous people. Identify the speaker using a speaker's tag (such as "Spielberg said," "According to Roberta Bondar," etc.). Choose your favourites, and post them on cards around the classroom or in your locker.

USAGE & STYLE

Be Able To

• use *accept* and *except* correctly

Except means to exclude or leave out. **Accept** means to take something offered.

All of the students in the class except Justin were busily writing away.

The teacher did not accept his excuse for not writing.

Unit **1** **Anecdote**

1. In your notebook, write the correct word *(accept* or *except)* for each of the blanks in the following anecdote.

> A tall young man was trying desperately to get a summer job. Everyone _____ Eugene seemed to be successful. He was at the point where he would _____ just about anything. Would they not _____ him because he was too tall? While swimming one evening he had an idea. "I'll apply to be a lifeguard at the swimming pool," he thought. He completed the application form in the usual fashion, _____ at the bottom of it he wrote: "Depth of swimming pool: six feet. Height of applicant: six feet three inches!"

2. Set aside part of your notebook for a section called WORDS I SOMETIMES CONFUSE. You will probably need to save four pages or so to use during the school year. Each time you learn about commonly confused words, write these words in your notebook, describe when to use them, and provide examples so you can refer to them quickly, if needed.

Techno Tip

If you can, try writing your list on a computer. That way you can keep the words in alphabetical order for easy reference.

SPELLING

Know

- some of the letter patterns that represent the long vowel sounds

There are a number of letter patterns that make long vowel sounds. Here are some common patterns, listed with the long vowel sound they can make.

a	e	i	o	u
a + e (cake)	ee (been)	i + e (bite)	o + e (hope)	u + e (huge)
ai (bait)	ea (each)	ie (pie)	oa (coat)	ew (threw)
ay (hay)	e (the)	igh (high)	oe (doe)	oo (school)
ea (steak)	ei (either)	y (why)	ou (boulder)	ou (soup)
eigh (eight)	ie (chief)	ye (goodbye)	ow (bowl)	u (unit)
ey (they)	y (lazy)			ue (blue)
				ui (fruit)

Words to Watch For

These words, taken from the anecdotes at the beginning of the unit, have at least one long vowel sound each.

famous	busily	lazily	threw	imitation
straight	cruelty	don't	simulate	identifying

In your notebook, make a list of 8-10 words that have a long vowel sound and that can be difficult to spell. You can use words from this box, the anecdotes, and your personal reading. To help you learn the words, underline the patterns that make the long vowel sounds.

1. Use the list, the anecdotes, or other reading materials to find words that contain these patterns and that make the long vowel sound indicated. Find four words for each pattern.

    a) **ai** (a)   b) **ea** (e)   c) **i + e** (i)   d) **oa** (o)   e) **ue** (u)

2. The **Words to Watch For** list contains synonyms and antonyms for each of the following words. For each synonym or antonym you identify, write a sentence in your notebook that shows its meaning.

    a) unkindness   b) crooked   c) unknown
    d) energetically   e) caught   f) copy

Strategy

Setting up a **Personal Dictionary** is an excellent way to improve your spelling. It is an ongoing list of words that you have trouble spelling. A two-column format is useful. Write the word in the left column, and in the right column include the word in a sentence to illustrate what it means. Keep your Personal Dictionary handy when you are proofreading.

Scroll Back

Edit and proofread the anecdote you drafted earlier, paying particular attention to the following checklist:

❏ Have you used specific nouns wherever possible?
❏ Are quotations punctuated and capitalized correctly?
❏ Are *accept* and *except*, or any other commonly confused words, used correctly?
❏ Have you spelled every word correctly, especially those that contain long vowel sounds?

Unit **1** **Anecdote**

Unit 2 Fable

What is a fable?

A fable is a short folktale that teaches a lesson or moral. Fables are usually about animals whose actions reflect human flaws and foolishness.

The Camel and the Mouse
by Rumi

One day an untended camel was approached by a mouse. "Let me lead you," the mouse said. Since the camel had nowhere to go and no one to protect him, he agreed to follow the mouse.

Taking the camel's halter in his hand, the mouse began to march the camel across the wilderness. It wasn't long before they came to a swift and angry river. The mouse pulled back from the shore, but the camel stepped into the water. It was up to his knees.

"Take me up on your shoulders and carry me across the river," the mouse commanded, "or I will drown."

"You should have thought of this before you tried to become a leader," the camel answered, and marched across the river by himself.

Know

- the characteristics of fables
- the function of pronouns
- what an antecedent is
- what gender bias is and some ways of avoiding it
- rules for punctuation and capitalization of split quotations
- patterns that make the **shun** sound

Be Able To

- write a fable
- identify antecedents of pronouns
- avoid some common problems in pronoun-antecedent agreement

The Oh So Grand Ox, and the Poor Pathetic Frog

by La Fontaine

One day an ox, having wandered far from his home, came to a pond that was filled with water lilies. He did not notice the croaking frog who was trying very hard to get his attention. Although the ox heard the croaking, he had no idea what it meant, or even who was doing it. He was too busy admiring the water lilies.

Meanwhile, the frog—who had never before seen a creature so large or majestic, so proud or mysterious, or so strange—found herself growing larger and larger in an attempt to be noticed. Croaking and puffing, and puffing and croaking, she sprang from her lily pad to the shore, but she still couldn't get the ox's attention.

Finally, the frog began rolling on her sides, and twisting her head this way and that, to see if she had been noticed, until her outer skin was so completely filled with hot air that she exploded.

The ox looked down to see what had made such a noise, but the frog of course was no longer there.

A Challenge

The moral of a fable is sometimes directly stated at the end of the story. Decide as a class how you would express the moral of each of the two model fables.

Checkpoint: Fable

Discuss how these characteristics of a fable apply to the models. Later, you can use the list to help you revise your own work.

✓ It is usually short and simple.

✓ The characters are often animals who act like humans.

✓ Everything in the story is designed to illustrate the moral.

✓ The ending makes the moral clear, either by directly stating it or by implication.

1. Check your school library for books of fables by Aesop, La Fontaine, or other writers. Read as many of these as you can to give you ideas for your own fables.

2. Before you start to write your fable, consider the following questions:

   · What setting will I use? (You can use a traditional or a modern setting.)
   · What proverb or moral will I use?
   · What animals will I use as characters?
   · What situation can I describe to illustrate my moral?

Idea File

You can either borrow one of the following morals, or make up one of your own.

Honesty is the best policy.

Necessity is the mother of invention.

Don't count your chickens before they hatch.

Writing

3. Write a draft of your fable. Make it short and keep it simple. End with a moral.

4. Refer back to the Checkpoint and revise your fable until you are satisfied with its focus, content, and organization.

GRAMMAR

Language
Link

Know
- the function of pronouns
- what an antecedent is

Be Able To
- identify antecedents of pronouns
- avoid some common problems in pronoun-antecedent agreement

A **pronoun** is a word that replaces a noun or another pronoun.

Pronouns help you to avoid unnecessary repetition in your writing. Imagine what this sentence would sound like without the pronouns in boldface.

> Since the camel had nowhere to go and no one to protect **him**, **he** agreed to follow the mouse.

An **antecedent** is a word that the pronoun stands for or replaces.

The antecedent is the noun the pronoun refers to.

antecedent   antecedent pronoun   pronoun

> Although the <u>ox</u> heard the <u>croaking</u>, <u>he</u> had no idea what <u>it</u> meant.

Pronouns must **agree** with their antecedents.

If the antecedent is singular, the pronoun must be singular as well. If the antecedent is plural, the pronoun must be plural. (The following two examples, and several others in this unit, are taken from the well-known fables of Aesop. Can you identify the fables?)

plural antecedent   plural pronoun

> The <u>mice</u> once held a meeting to discuss how to outwit <u>their</u> enemy, the cat.

singular pronoun   singular antecedent

> Confident of <u>his</u> greater speed, the <u>hare</u> was in no hurry.

1. Identify the antecedent for each of the pronouns in boldface, and tell whether it is singular or plural.

   a) One fine day in winter, the ants were busy drying **their** store of corn.

   b) The lion was so tickled at the idea of the mouse being able to help **him**, that **he** lifted up **his** paw and let **him** go.

Unit **2** Fable

Usually, you will have no trouble figuring out the correct pronoun to use. However, be careful in sentences that contain prepositional phrases near the subject.

For more on prepositional phrases, see Unit 12.

subject   prepositional phrase   pronoun

<u>Each</u>   <u>of the boys</u> had   <u>his</u> own hideout.

In this case, the antecedent of **his** is *each [boy]*, not *boys*.

Also remember that antecedents like *anyone, someone, anybody, somebody,* or *whoever* are all singular, and require a singular pronoun.

> **Somebody** forgot **his or her** book in the auditorium.

2. In your notebook, rewrite the following sentences, correcting any mistakes in the use of pronouns. Underline the antecedent of each pronoun.

    a) The fables and legends of a country tell a lot about their culture.
    b) Most people have read his or her share of *Aesop's Fables*.
    c) Many fables trace its origin to the *Fables of Bidpai*.
    d) Bidpai, a sage of India, used fables to instruct the princes of its land.

3. Check through several pieces of writing you have already completed, and correct any errors you made in pronoun-antecedent agreement.

Language Link

MECHANICS

Know
- rules for punctuation and capitalization of split quotations

> "Take me up on your shoulders and carry me across the river," the mouse commanded, "or I will drown."

> "Madam Crow, I've heard that your voice is beyond compare," said the fox. "Wouldn't you just sing a few notes for me?"

Splitting a quotation into two parts, as in the two examples above, is a good way to vary the rhythm of your sentences.

1. Based on the examples above, develop a set of rules to explain how to punctuate and capitalize split quotations. Make sure you answer all of the following questions in your rules.

    • How many sets of quotation marks are used in split quotations?
    • What punctuation mark is used at the end of the first part of the quotation?

- When are capitals used in a split quotation?
- Is the punctuation mark placed before or after the closing quotation marks?

2. Apply your rules to the split quotations in the fable below. Rewrite each split quotation in your notebook in its correct form.

The Wolf and the Lamb
by Aesop

A thirsty wolf and a thirsty lamb came to the same stream to drink. Upstream stood the wolf; farther down stood the lamb. But the wolf, who had a taste for tender young meat, was not about to let the lamb be.

"Why?" said he. "Have you muddied the water where I'm drinking"?

"How could I? answered the lamb, The water flows downstream from you to me."

"Hmpf." said the wolf, quiet for a moment. "But why did you curse me, six months back"?

How could I? answered the lamb. Six months ago I wasn't even born.

"Well", the wolf went on. "If it wasn't you, it must have been your father"!

And with that he pounced upon the lamb and ate him up.

MORAL: For a scoundrel, any excuse will do!

3. Do you have trouble punctuating quotations? Check through one piece of writing in which you used quotations or dialogue, correcting any errors you discover.

USAGE & STYLE

Know
- what gender bias is and some ways of avoiding it

Gender bias occurs when writers use only masculine (or only feminine) terms as if they were neutral. Writing that displays gender bias can create a false impression that either females or males are being excluded. In many older works, including some fables, it was considered acceptable to use a masculine pronoun or the word "man" to represent people generally. Today, however, most writers want to avoid gender bias, and so they choose their language carefully.

Biased:	Whoever lost **his** jacket can pick it up at the office.
Neutral:	Whoever lost **a** jacket can pick it up at the office.
	Whoever lost **his or her** jacket can pick it up at the office.

Biased:	**He** who laughs last, laughs best.
Neutral:	**They** who laugh last, laugh best.
	The one who laughs last, laughs best.

In speech, we often avoid the pronoun problem by substituting a plural pronoun *(they, them,* or *their)* for *he, him,* or *his.* For example,

> Whoever lost **their** jacket can pick it up at the office.

But, since this breaks the rule about pronouns agreeing with their antecedents, it is not acceptable in written work. Use one of the other methods listed above, or reword the sentence entirely.

1. Find a new way to express each of the following to avoid the problem of gender bias. (Change words as well as pronouns, where necessary.)

   a) Nobody believes a liar, even when he tells the truth.
   b) Man has yet to make a better mousetrap.
   c) A man can't have his cake and eat it too.

SPELLING

Know
- patterns that make the **shun** sound

There are a number of patterns that can make the sound of **shun**, including *tion, tian, sion, sian, cion,* and *cian.* There are a few rules that can help you spell some words that end with the **shun** sound.

- In most words, the **shun** sound is made by the *tion* pattern.
- Words that end in the sound **ashun** are usually made by the pattern *ation.*
- Career names, like *physician,* sometimes end in *cian.*
- Names of residents (for example, *Nova Scotian*) sometimes end in *tian* or *sian.*

Words to Watch For

All of these words end with the **shun** sound. The first one is taken from the fable at the beginning of the unit. The others are words you might use in your own fable or other writings.

attention   expedition   transportation   admiration   production
protection   destination   permission   introduction   explosion

In your notebook, make a list of 8-10 words that end with the **shun** sound. You can use words from this box and your personal reading.

1. Complete the chart in your notebook by filling in the missing words.

Root	+ s	+ ed	+ ing	+ **sion** or **tion** or **ation**
protect		protected		
transport			transporting	
permit	permits			
attend		attended		
explode			exploding	

2. Look at the final consonant of each root word in the chart. In which root words does the final consonant change when the **shun** pattern is added? In your notebook, write other root words that change in the same way. Find two examples of each change.

3. Challenge a partner. Time yourself for five minutes. List as many career names as you can that end in *cian*, and as many names of residents (of cities or countries) that end in *sian*. At the end of five minutes compare lists. How many of the same names did you list?

Scroll Back

Edit and proofread your fable, paying particular attention to the following:

❑ Do all the pronouns agree with their antecedents?
❑ Are quotations punctuated and capitalized correctly?
❑ Have you avoided gender bias in your use of pronouns?
❑ Are all words spelled correctly? Pay special attention to words that contain the **shun** sound.

Unit **2** Fable

Unit 3 Autobiography

What is an autobiography?

An autobiography is the story of someone's life, as told by the person him- or herself. Autobiographies may include stories about major events in a person's life (such as births, deaths, and marriages). However, they also may contain stories about less important events, which reveal something significant about the author's life or personality. The following story is taken from *Little by Little*, the autobiography of the author Jean Little.

In the fall I went into Miss Ibbotson's class. We had to learn about decimals and percents. I disliked [that year in school] till the day Miss Ibbotson started us writing journals.

When she passed out the notebooks, they did not look special. They had blue paper covers and lined pages with a thin red margin. I could not see those faint lines when I was writing.

"For the last half hour, every day this month," Miss Ibbotson told us, "you will keep a diary. You will write in them what happened in your life that day and how you felt."

She talked on for a few minutes, but I was not listening. I could hardly wait to begin.

That first afternoon, I did write down what had actually happened in my life that day. I may even have stuck to the truth till page three or four. But long before the first week was up, I had begun fancying things up a little. My real life was simply too dull to be worth recording.

I began stealing ideas from a book we had at home called *Boyhood Stories of Famous Men*. In the book one boy saved the day by carving a lion out of butter to be used as a decoration for the King's table. Another made his own paints by crushing berries and boiling roots, and little Wolfgang Mozart and his big sister went to perform on the harpsichord before the child Marie Antoinette. The book went on to explain how each boy later became famous.

Know

- the characteristics of an autobiography
- the rules for capitalization
- alternatives for the word *said*
- how new words can be made by adding prefixes and suffixes to root words

Be Able To

- write an incident for your own autobiography
- form the possessives of singular and plural nouns

I liked the story about the young Mozart best. What drew me to it was his older sister. She was shown in the illustration, standing behind Wolfgang and the pretty little princess. I knew exactly how she must be feeling. She, too, was a gifted musician, but her little brother was the hero of the story. It never said what happened to her.

In my journal, I had myself carving wonderful animals, playing the piano brilliantly before I was five and making my own paints.

One day's entry read like this:

Last night, a famous artist came to have supper at our house. Mother took him down to the cellar. The great painter stopped dead in his tracks and pointed to our cellar walls.

"Madam," he cried, "whoever painted these magnificent murals on your walls?"

Mother stared at the wondrous paintings.

"I have no idea," she said in a bewildered voice. She turned to her children.

"Children," she said, "have you any idea who painted these magnificent murals?"

The other children shook their heads.

"As a matter of fact," I said, "I painted them."

"But you had no paints!" Mother cried.

"I know," I said modestly, "but I so longed to paint that I boiled roots and squeezed berries and made my own paints."

The great artist patted my head.

"Madam," he said, with tears in his eyes, "someday this little girl of yours will be world famous as an artist."

WRITER'S WORKSHOP

Checkpoint: Autobiography

Discuss how these characteristics of an autobiography apply to the model. Later, you can use the list to help you revise your own autobiographical incident.

✓ It is written in the first person (I).

✓ It is a true story, based on events in the writer's own life.

✓ It is usually written in chronological order.

✓ It tells about important people, places, events, and phases in a person's life.

✓ It reveals something about the author's feelings, values, and ambitions.

1. Begin by dividing your life into phases. For example, you might divide it into babyhood, childhood, and early teen years. Or the divisions might be preschool, elementary school, and junior high school. Or, you might decide that the phases will relate to important events in your life. For example, if you moved to Canada from another country, you might decide that the move marked a new phase in your life.

2. Since you will not have time to write about all the phases of your life, choose one, and in the middle of a new page in your notebook give the phase a name or short title. Then create a web that lists events, incidents, and any other details you can think of that would help to describe your life during that phase. Here is an example of part of a web:

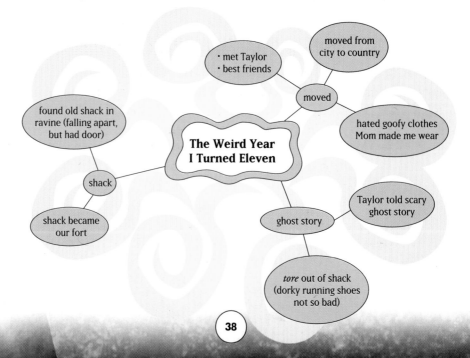

3. From your web, choose the events and information that you think are the most important. Limit yourself to one or two incidents or events that best reveal what your life was like, or what you were like, at that time.

4. Arrange the parts of your story in a logical order. Then write a first draft.

5. Refer back to the Checkpoint, and revise your draft until you are satisfied with its focus, content, and organization.

GRAMMAR

Be Able To
- form the possessives of singular and plural nouns

A **possessive noun** is a noun that indicates who or what owns something.

To form the possessive of most singular nouns, add an apostrophe (') and **s**.

     Miss Ibbotson's class   the King's table   one day's entry

To form the possessive of a plural noun that does not end in **s**, add an apostrophe (') and **s**.

     people's autobiographies   men's lives   geese's teeth

To form the possessive of a plural noun that ends in **s**, add just an apostrophe (').

     the berries' stems   the Littles' daughter   the murals' effect

1. Rewrite each of the following sentences in your notebook using a possessive noun. (For example, *the colours of the paints* would become *the paints' colours*.)

   a)   The covers of the notebooks were made of blue paper.
   b)   The diaries contained the feelings of the students.
   c)   By the end of the week, Jean was inventing stories.
   d)   One of the sisters of Wolfgang Amadeus was mentioned in the book.
   e)   The childhoods of the boys were remarkable.

Strategy

Remember that most words that end in **s** do NOT need any apostrophe at all. Before you add one, make sure the word is possessive, not just plural (or a singular noun that ends in **s**).

2. Correct any errors in the use of possessives or plurals in the following passage. Write the corrected words in your notebook.

> Jean Little was born in Taiwan, where her parent's were missionary's. Upon their return to Canada, Jeans' family settled in Guelph, Ontario.
> The Little's were very supportive of their daughter, who had a visual disability from birth, and later lost all her vision. Jean's brother's names were Hugh and Jamie. Her sisters' name was Pat.
> Jean graduated from the University of Torontos Victoria College in 1955, and has gone on to become one of the countrys best-loved childrens' writer's.

When more than one person or thing share a single possession, add an apostrophe and **s** to the last noun in the series.

> Wolfgang and his sister's concert

When possession is not shared by each noun in the series, form the possessive in the regular way.

> The painter's, the sculptor's, and the musician's childhoods.

3. Rewrite the following expressions in your notebook, using the correct possessive form (for example, *the sounds of the harpsichord and piano* would become *the harpsichord's and piano's sounds*).

   a) the table of the king and queen
   b) the imaginations of the brother and sister
   c) the colours of the berries and roots

4. Write a list of possessive nouns that describe you. Examples might be: *my mother's daughter, nobody's fool, Susan's brother,* etc. When you have written as many as you can, check your use of apostrophes, then arrange the list in an order that suits you, and put your name at the top. You will have created an autobiographical poem.

MECHANICS

Know
- the rules for capitalization

Throughout the writing of your autobiography, you probably used capital letters for the names of people, places, and perhaps events.

1. The list on the next page indicates some of the kinds of words that should be capitalized. Illustrate each rule with a sentence that tells about yourself (for example, your name, date of birth, clubs you belong to, products you like or use).

Capitalize ...
- proper nouns
- proper adjectives
- religions, nationalities, and languages
- titles used with names
- days and months
- geographical names
- first words at the beginning of sentences or direct quotations
- historical events, documents, or periods of time
- abbreviations
- organizations
- names of products

2. Did any of these rules surprise you? Choose three pieces of writing you have completed and check them to see if you have forgotten to use capitals anywhere. Choose the three rules you think you are most likely to forget, and write three more examples for each.

Techno Tip

It's easy to miss capitalizing when you are typing fast on a computer. Check that the first words of sentences are capitalized by searching for periods. Then do an individual check for every proper name you know you used in your piece. Finally, proofread your work yourself to check for words you may have missed.

USAGE & STYLE

"Madam," **he cried**, "whoever painted these magnificent murals on your walls?"

Using dialogue is a good way to add interest to your autobiography. Like all use of detail, it makes your description of an event more vivid and convincing.

Know
- alternatives for the word *said*

Words like "he said" or "she exclaimed" are called **speaker's tags**. When writing dialogue, try to avoid overusing the word *said* in speaker's tags. Each of the words below adds its own shade of meaning. For example, *commanded* implies greater feeling or purpose than *requested*. *Giggled* is somewhat different from *laughed*.

accused	coaxed	faltered	laughed
admitted	commanded	gasped	moaned
advised	complained	giggled	noted
agreed	confessed	hinted	objected
asserted	countered	implied	requested
barked	declared	inquired	snapped
bellowed	demanded	insisted	snickered
charged	droned	interrupted	warned

1. Replace the words *said* and *cried* in Jean Little's journal entry with words that add appropriate shades of meaning to the dialogue.

A Challenge

Write your own puns using speaker's tags that relate to various occupations or situations, as in the following examples:

"The engine's dying!" sputtered the pilot.

"I'll get that cockroach," fumed the exterminator.

2. Choose a piece of writing containing dialogue that you have written this year. Change any speaker's tags that you think could be improved.

SPELLING

Know

- how new words can be made by adding prefixes and suffixes to root words

A root word is a word (or word part) that prefixes and suffixes are added to, and in this way new words are created. Both prefixes and suffixes change a word's meaning.

- A prefix can change a word to its opposite:
  like → **dis**like   stuck → **un**stuck
- A suffix can change a verb from present to past tense:
  explain → explain**ed**
- A suffix can change a verb to a noun:
  perform → perform**ance**

Words to Watch For

These are words you might use in your autobiographical incident. All of them contain a root to which a prefix or a suffix has been added. Some have been taken from the story by Jean Little at the beginning of the unit.

disliked	uninteresting	decoration	musician	bewildered
happened	factual	illustration	wondrous	celebrated

In your notebook, make a list of 8-10 words that contain a root word and a prefix and/or a suffix. You can use words from this box, the excerpt from Jean Little's autobiography, and your own reading.

1. In your notebook, write the root of each word in your list.

2. "Explode" two **Words to Watch For**. Do this by writing the root of each lesson word, then as many words as you can that share the same root.

Strategy

Adding a prefix or a suffix usually does not change the spelling of the root, or changes it very little. Focus on the root when learning to spell words that have a prefix or a suffix. The next time you have to spell the word, think of the root and then add the prefix or suffix.

3. Which **Words to Watch For** are synonyms or antonyms of these words?

   a) liked   b) dull   c) magical   d) fictional
   e) artist   f) enjoyed   g) picture   h) confused

4. Many words we use today come from Latin and Greek roots. For example, the word *autobiography* is a combination of three Greek root words. *Auto* means "self" or "same"; *bio* means "life"; and *graph* means "to write." Find three other words that are made from a combination of two or more Greek or Latin root words. Show what each root is and tell what it means.

Scroll Back

Edit and proofread your autobiographical incident, paying particular attention to the following:

❏ Have you formed possessives properly?
❏ Have you capitalized words correctly?
❏ Have you used appropriate alternatives for the word *said* in your speaker's tags?
❏ Have you spelled all words correctly, especially those that contain prefixes and/or suffixes?

Unit **3**   **Autobiography**

Unit (4) Friendly Letter or E-Mail

What is a friendly letter?

A friendly letter is a letter (or e-mail) written to someone you know personally. There are many reasons for writing a friendly letter — to thank or congratulate someone, to apologize or express sympathy, or just to share some news.

228 Fairlane Cres. } Return Address
Vancouver, B.C.
V6C 3X5

August 3, 1998 ← Date

← Salutation

Dear Sunil,

> We visited the Vancouver Aquarium today and it was awesome! I laughed at the sea otters. I ogled the killer whales. I got lost in a kelp forest...It's true! They had to call my name over the loudspeakers before we were reunited. It was so embarrassing. I felt like a five year old (especially after I bought a goofy souvenir for $2.50).
> We've been in Vancouver for six days now, and there are two weeks left before we fly the 2312 kilometres (!) back home. About 80 percent of our time has been spent visiting relatives, taking in the sights, and eating—mostly fish.
> Twelve hours from now we plan on taking the ferry to Victoria. It's supposed to be 18°C, but sunny. Unfortunately, we have to get up at 5:30 a.m. to catch the ferry. Yikes! — Body

Your best friend, } Closing

Moira

P.S. I'm sending this by snail mail because I forgot to bring your e-mail address with me. Could you send it to me? You can e-mail me at my uncle's address: nomsing@wilson.net.

At the end of this unit you will

Know

- the features of a friendly letter
- the rules for writing numbers
- the difference between informal and formal usage
- consonant patterns that form digraphs, and the sound each digraph makes

Be Able To

- write a friendly letter
- use conjunctions to combine sentences
- adjust the formality of your writing

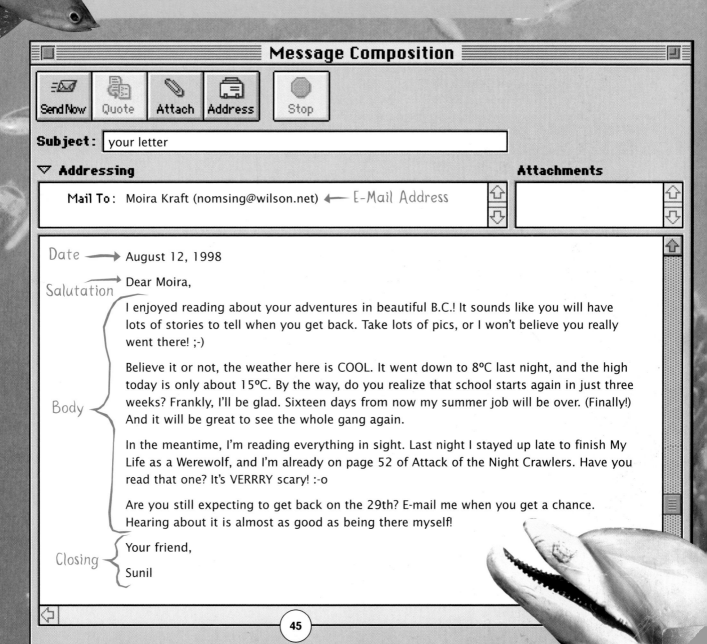

Message Composition

Send Now Quote Attach Address Stop

Subject: your letter

▽ **Addressing**   **Attachments**

Mail To: Moira Kraft (nomsing@wilson.net) ← E-Mail Address

Date → August 12, 1998

Salutation → Dear Moira,

I enjoyed reading about your adventures in beautiful B.C.! It sounds like you will have lots of stories to tell when you get back. Take lots of pics, or I won't believe you really went there! ;-)

Believe it or not, the weather here is COOL. It went down to 8ºC last night, and the high today is only about 15ºC. By the way, do you realize that school starts again in just three weeks? Frankly, I'll be glad. Sixteen days from now my summer job will be over. (Finally!) And it will be great to see the whole gang again.

Body

In the meantime, I'm reading everything in sight. Last night I stayed up late to finish My Life as a Werewolf, and I'm already on page 52 of Attack of the Night Crawlers. Have you read that one? It's VERRRY scary! :-o

Are you still expecting to get back on the 29th? E-mail me when you get a chance. Hearing about it is almost as good as being there myself!

Closing → Your friend,

Sunil

45

WRITER'S WORKSHOP

Checkpoint: Friendly Letter/E-Mail

Discuss how the following general characteristics of a friendly letter or e-mail apply to the models. Later, you can use the list to help you revise your own work.

✓ It is written in the first person.

✓ It usually uses fairly informal language.

✓ It has a conversational tone.

✓ It begins with a salutation, and ends with a closing that includes your name. Sometimes there is a return address as well.

1. Decide who you will write to. Make your recipient a person you know or would like to know, rather than a business. Will you use e-mail or regular mail?

Techno Tip

"I'm having a party!" If you have e-mail, you can send the same message to a number of people at the same time. To make this easier, you can also set up your own electronic "address book."

2. Jot down a list of topics you want to talk about before you start to write.

3. Before you start to write, think of words, phrases, or ideas to connect your topics. Then write a first draft, using these words, phrases, or ideas to guide you. If you have trouble getting started, try

   · responding to something from an earlier letter
   · describing your surroundings or mood
   · launching right into an exciting event
   · sharing a joke or asking a question

4. Decide if you need to add or delete anything. Refer back to the Checkpoint, and revise your letter accordingly.

GRAMMAR

A **conjunction** is a word that joins words or groups of words, as in the following examples.

We've been in Vancouver for six days now, **and** it's still hard to believe that long 2312-kilometre trip is over.

They had to call my name over the loudspeakers **before** we were reunited.

Conjunctions help join related ideas together so that your writing flows more smoothly. Here is a list of some of the more common conjunctions:

but	and	or	whether	unless
since	yet	while	that	than
if	because	for	yet	so
as	neither	until	through	when
	nor			while

1. In your notebook, combine each of the following pairs of sentences into one sentence using a conjunction. Try to use a different conjunction for each pair.

   a) I laughed at the sea otters. I ogled the killer whales.
   b) It was so embarrassing. I felt like I was five years old again.
   c) Tomorrow we are going to Granville Island. It has a farmer's market.

2. Write five sentences, each one containing a conjunction from the list of common conjunctions above. Can you write an additional sentence that uses two (or more!) conjunctions?

3. By combining sentences, you can change the tone, or feeling, of your writing.

   • A series of short sentences can help build suspense.
   • A short sentence following several long ones will add emphasis.
   • Long sentences can create a relaxed, slow, or thoughtful mood.

   Experiment with a piece of your own writing, identifying places where you could make it more effective by shortening or lengthening sentences.

Language Link

MECHANICS

Know

• the rules for writing numbers

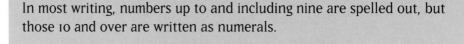

In most writing, numbers up to and including nine are spelled out, but those 10 and over are written as numerals.

There are **two** weeks left before we fly the **2312** kilometres (!) back home.

1. Every rule has exceptions, however. Make a list of all the numbers that appear as numerals in the two models. With a group, compile a list of exceptions to the rule, along with examples from the models. Use a chart like the one below:

Use numerals for	Example
Dates	*August 3, 1998*

2. Write another rule about numbers that appear as the first word of a sentence.

3. Look back at three of your recent pieces of writing. Make changes to any numbers that you may have written incorrectly.

4. Working with a partner, make up 10 sentences using numbers in various situations. (Use only one number in each sentence.) Read your sentences to another pair of students, and have them write the numbers. Reverse roles, then score your results.

USAGE & STYLE

Would you dress up for a baseball game? Probably not. Different situations require different levels of formality. This goes not only for clothes, but also for the level of language you use. Language can range from very informal to very formal. The level you use in your writing depends on your purpose and your audience.

1. Working alone or with a partner, make a list of the differences between the two letters below.

Know
- the difference between informal and formal usage

Be Able To
- adjust the formality of your writing

Informal

> HEY JOE!
>
> I CAN'T BELIEVE IT! I WON'T BE ABLE TO MAKE IT TO YOUR PARTY ON SAT. BECAUSE I'VE GOTTA WORK, AND NO ONE WILL TAKE OVER MY SHIFT. I'VE TRIED EVERYONE A MILLION TIMES. No LUCK. SORRY, BUD, BUT MAYBE WE COULD HANG OUT TOGETHER ON SUN.
>
> TALK TO YOU THEN,
>
> ALI

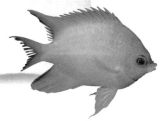

Formal

> Dear Joe,
>
> I regret to inform you that I will not be able to attend your party next Saturday night. I am scheduled to work that evening, and have been unsuccessful in convincing a coworker to switch shifts with me, despite numerous entreaties. Please accept my sincere apologies. Perhaps, instead, we could rendezvous on Sunday?
>
> I hope to speak with you soon.
>
> Regards,
>
> Ali

Unit 4 **Friendly Letter or E-Mail**

Summarize your responses under the following headings:

Words Used	Length of Sentences	Tone

2. Write two brief letters, one formal and the other informal. Make sure that you use contrasting tones in each letter.

SPELLING

Know

- consonant patterns that form digraphs, and the sound each digraph makes

A **digraph** is two consonants that combine to make one sound. The first paragraph of Moira's letter contains examples of three digraphs (**th**, **ch**, and **sh**), and there are three others as well (**wh**, **ph**, and **gh**).

th	ch	sh	wh	ph	gh
there	each	fish	which	phone	tough

- Digraphs can occur at any point in a word—beginning, middle, and end;
- **ch, sh,** and **th** make a new sound;
- **wh** usually makes the sound of **w**, but can also make the sound of **h** (whole);
- **ph** and **gh** make the sound of **f** (laugh), but **gh** can also be silent (daughter);
- the sound of **sh** and **ch** digraphs can be made by other letter combinations, for example, **s** (sure), **ti** (accommodation, question).

 ## Words to Watch For

These words contain digraphs. Some have been taken from the models; others have been added to represent all of the digraphs.

champion	photograph	bought	finish	rhythm
whatever	worth	whole	everything	schedule

In your notebook, make a list of 8-10 words containing digraphs that can be difficult to spell. Use words from this box, the letters, or your personal reading. To help you learn the words, circle the digraph(s) in each one.

1. Use your word list, personal dictionary, and books you are reading to find four examples of each digraph. Write the words in your notebook.

   a) ch   b) sh   c) th
   d) wh   e) gh (f)   f) gh (silent)   g) ph

2. Use words from **Words to Watch For** to complete these phrases.

   a) _____ and sold
   b) whenever, _____
   c) one who has triumphed, a _____
   d) value _____
   e) _____ of a song
   f) work _____

Strategy

You probably have difficulty with only one or two letters in each of your list words. Try circling these letters. The next time you write the word, close your eyes and "see" the circled letters. Write what you see in your mind.

---

3. Choose five of your list words. Write a synonym for each word. Give your synonyms and word list to a partner. Can she or he make the right matches?

4. **Ti** and **s** are two of six patterns that make the sound of the **sh** digraph. Work with a partner to list the other patterns. Give an example word for each. How many patterns did you identify? Compare your work with that of another pair of students.

5. Make a crossword puzzle in which each answer contains at least one digraph. Write your answers on the back of your puzzle and place it with puzzles your classmates have completed. Try completing a classmate's puzzle.

Scroll Back

Edit and proofread your letter, paying particular attention to the following checklist:

❑ Is the level of language suitable for your purpose and audience?
❑ Does your writing flow? (Have you used a combination of long and short sentences?)
❑ Have you followed the rules for writing numbers?
❑ Are all words with a digraph spelled correctly? (Are all other words from your list spelled correctly?)

Description

"It looked like ...."

"It sounded like ...."

Whether the subject is a person, place, object, or even an idea, description involves choosing details that convey a specific impression. For example, you're likely to describe your favourite music video using words that convey a particular image, while your parents or grandparents might choose words that convey quite a different image.

This section contains four forms of descriptive writing: setting description, comparison, travelogue, and descriptive poetry. Through careful selection and presentation of details, each piece paints a vivid impression of its subject, helping us to experience things in new ways.

Features of Description

- Descriptions focus on creating a dominant impression of a subject.

- Descriptive writers try to choose words, images, and details that appeal to more than one sense.

- Descriptive writing often uses figurative language techniques such as simile and metaphor.

- Descriptions of people, places, and things are often organized spatially (for example, left to right, top to bottom) or by features (for example, from most to least noticeable).

Unit 5 Setting Description

What is a setting description?

A setting description is a description of a place. It may stand on its own, form part of a more general descriptive passage, or be used to set the scene for a narrative. The following setting description is taken from *The Root Cellar*, a novel by Janet Lunn.

Downstairs was like turning on a radio and getting all the stations at once. The television was going in the living room. George was perched on one arm of the sofa making running comments as he watched. Aunt Nan was beating something with an electric beater in the kitchen and talking in a loud voice to someone who made an occasional rumbling response. In sing-song voices the twins were anxiously telling their mother, "We don't want any peas, we don't want any peas."

Rose stood at the foot of the stairs trying to take it all in. The living room was in worse condition than her bedroom. It was a large room full of doors and windows, cluttered with furniture that appeared to have been left wherever the moving men had deposited it a month earlier. The bare lath was exposed through large holes in the walls. She couldn't understand why the front room upstairs had been made so charming while the living room was in such a state.

At the end of this unit you will

Know

- the characteristics of a setting description
- the main types of verbs
- some common compound words

Be Able To

- write a setting description
- use commas in a series correctly
- create rhythm and variety in your writing

She went through into the kitchen which was much more cheerful. It had been scrubbed and repaired. Along one wall there was a big old fireplace with a bake oven beside it. The other walls and the low ceiling were a honey-coloured wood that reflected softly the light from the fire burning in the fireplace and from the lamps on the mantel and the small table under the front window. Against the back wall was a big brown electric range, counters (obviously new) and a sink with small square windows over it. There were shelves for dishes over the windows—but most of the dishes were on the big table in the middle of the room or piled up dirty in the sink. An old wooden rocking-chair stood by the front window, covered—as was every other possible space—with books, magazines, rubber boots and sweaters.

WRITER'S WORKSHOP

Checkpoint: Setting Description

Discuss how these characteristics of a setting description apply to the model. Later, you can use the list to help you revise your own work.

✓ The setting may be described from left to right, top to bottom, etc., or it may move from an overall impression to focus on specific details.

✓ It often contains details designed to create a certain mood or atmosphere.

✓ It often contains details that appeal to the different senses.

✓ It is usually written from the narrator's point of view.

1. Identify a setting. It might be your classroom, a room in your home, a place you like, or a setting used in one of your writing pieces this year.

2. Draw a chart in your notebook like the one shown below. Complete as many sections as possible with words or phrases that describe your setting.

Sight	Sound	Smell	Touch	Taste

3. Decide how you will organize your description. Will you start from the top and move down, or will you move from left to right? Will you begin with a general impression, and then identify specific details? If so, how will the details be arranged?

4. Write a first draft of your setting description. Then revise it until you are satisfied with its focus, content, and organization.

GRAMMAR

Know

- the main types of verbs

A **verb** is a word that indicates an action or state of being.

There are three types of verbs: action, linking, and helping.

Action verbs tell what someone or something is doing. The activity can be physical or mental.

Physical Action: Rose **stood** at the foot of the stairs trying to take it all in.

Mental Action: She couldn't **understand** why the front room upstairs had been made so charming while the living room was in such a state.

1. Read the following sentences from the writing model in this unit. Write the action verbs for each of these sentences in your notebook.

   a) Aunt Nan was beating something with an electric beater in the kitchen and talking in a loud voice to someone who made an occasional rumbling response.
   b) She went through into the kitchen which was much more cheerful.

Linking verbs join a noun or pronoun to another word that describes it. The most common linking verb is **be**.

It **was** a large room full of doors and windows.

The linking verb *was* joins the pronoun *it* to the words *a large room*, which describe what *it* is.

Common forms of the linking verb *be*: *is, am, are, be, was, were*

Other verbs that can be linking verbs: *smell, look, taste, remain, become, feel, seem, sound, stay, appear, grow, turn*

2. Write the linking verbs for each sentence below in your notebook.

   a) The living room was in worse condition than her bedroom.
   b) The kitchen had been scrubbed and repaired so it looked much more cheerful.
   c) Downstairs felt like turning on a radio and getting all the stations at once.

Helping verbs help other verbs (main verbs) do their jobs. They help state an action or show time.

Unit **5** Setting Description

Helping verbs always come before the main verb.

helping verb   main verb   helping verb main verb

She <u>couldn't</u> <u>understand</u> why the front room upstairs <u>had been</u> <u>made</u> so charming.

Some verbs that can be helping verbs: *be, being, been, am, are, is, was, were, shall, will, could, would, should, may, might, must, have, has, do, did, does*

3. Read the following sentences from *The Root Cellar* excerpt. Write the helping verb and the main verb in your notebook.

   a) The television was going in the living room.
   b) She could see the bare lath through the large holes that had been made in the wall.
   c) The dishes that should have been put away were piled up on the table, which was in the middle of the room.

4. In your notebook write three headings: ACTION, LINKING, and HELPING. Under the appropriate heading write each of the verbs in the following passage (from another chapter of *The Root Cellar*).

   At the top of the steps she found herself standing beside a little garden with rows of young plants set out in it. Behind it the creek bubbled merrily and a stone path led from the garden to the kitchen floor. Pansies and sweet alyssum bloomed along the walk and there were hollyhocks against the back wall of the house. The bricks looked bright and the trim around the windows and the kitchen door was fresh and white. Chickens and ducks were squawking and flapping to let her know she was intruding, and a pair of geese scurried across the grass toward her.

5. Look through your draft of the setting description and identify all the action, linking, and helping verbs. Consider whether you have made the best use of action verbs possible to add strength to your description. Can you change any linking verbs to action verbs? If so, try it out and see which version you prefer.

MECHANICS

When you are writing a description of a setting, you may find yourself listing a series of objects or locations. If so, be aware of the rule for using commas in a series.

> Use a comma (,) to take the place of the word *and* when three or more things are listed together in a sentence.

> An old wooden rocking-chair stood by the front window, covered with **books, magazines, rubber boots, and sweaters**.

1. Rewrite the following sentences using commas correctly. Leave out the word *and* whenever possible.

   a) The television was going in the living room and George was perched on one arm of the sofa and Aunt Nan was beating something with an electric beater.

   b) The room was large and full of doors and windows and cluttered with furniture.

   c) The kitchen had been cleaned and scrubbed and repaired.

2. In your notebook draw four triangles. Inside each write the name of a place with which you are familiar. On each of the points of the triangle write a word or phrase that describes the place, as shown in the sample below. Use these three words or phrases in a sentence describing the place. Make sure you punctuate your sentences correctly.

Writing

three-storey

house

big   old

I live in a big, old, three-storey house.

Unit 5   Setting Description

USAGE & STYLE

Be Able To

- create rhythm and variety in your writing

Most writers try to vary the rhythm of their writing in order to keep the reader interested. Writers create variety by

- using a mix of short and long sentences
- varying the location of phrases and other modifiers, so that sentences do not always start with a subject and verb
- combining sentences
- finding synonyms for words that are repeated often
- replacing linking verbs with more expressive action verbs

1. Explain why the second group of sentences below is better than the first.

   On the left was the fridge. Beside the fridge was a big stove. Beside the stove was a counter.

   On the left stood the fridge. Beside that was a big stove with a counter next to it.

2. With a partner or on your own, revise the following passage to improve its rhythm and sentence variety.

   To the left of the entranceway was a door. It led into the living room. Inside the doorway on the opposite wall there was a large fireplace with an elaborate mantel around it. It dominated the room. Above the mantel was an old framed picture. It looked as if it hadn't been dusted in years. On either side of the fireplace were two grey couches. They looked like sentinels guarding an unknown treasure.

A Challenge

Repetition is not always undesirable. Repeating a word or using several sentences that begin in a similar way can help to draw a connection between sentences that are related. Can you find an example of this technique in the model description? Why do you think the author used repetition in this way?

3. Sometimes it can be hard to hear the rhythm of your own writing. Try having a partner read your draft of a setting description aloud. Listen for parts where the rhythm sounds uneven or inappropriate. Use the techniques listed earlier to revise the problem areas.

SPELLING

A compound word contains two words that have been combined to make one new word. The meaning of the new word is a blend of the two meanings. For example, *upstairs* contains *up* and *stairs* and means "up the stairs."

It is important to write all letters in both words. Only a few compound words drop one letter, and most of these include the word *all*. In these words (*always* is one example) one *l* is dropped.

Words to Watch For

All of these words are compound words. Some have been taken from the novel extract at the beginning of the unit. The others are the kind of words you might use in a setting description.

downstairs	upstairs	fireplace	everywhere	nowhere
doorway	bedroom	household	somewhere	anywhere

In your notebook, make a list of 8-10 compound words. You can use words from this box, the novel extract, and your reading.

1. Underline the two words that make up each compound word in your list.

2. Words like *where, some,* and *any* are common in compound words. Write as many words as you can that include these words.

3. Work with a partner. Make a list of compound words classified under these headings: HOUSEHOLD TERMS, FOOD TERMS, DIRECTION TERMS, and TIME TERMS. Then use each of these words in a sentence. Try to make this sentence as vividly descriptive as you can.

Scroll Back

Edit and proofread your setting description, paying particular attention to the following checklist:

- ❏ Have you appealed to as many senses as possible in your description?
- ❏ Have you included some action verbs to strengthen your writing?
- ❏ Have you varied the rhythm of your sentences?
- ❏ Have you used commas properly when listing items in a series?
- ❏ Are all words spelled correctly, particularly compound words?

Unit (6) Comparison

What is a comparison?

Comparison is a powerful writing technique used in English, science, geography, and many other subjects. By identifying the common features of two or more persons, places, actions, or things, and then describing how these features differ, a comparison allows the reader to understand a topic more clearly. In the following article, Mike Fabbro compares skiing to snowboarding.

I never fully appreciated the popularity of snowboarding with kids until I saw two young boys—one a skier, the other a snowboarder—walking through the village at Mont Tremblant. The skier looked frustrated as he trudged along in his huge ski boots, buckles undone for flexibility, occasionally sliding on ice. In his one-piece, Barney-purple ski suit, he clutched his skis and poles in a desperate attempt not to drop them. He just didn't look like a happy little camper.

The snowboarder, on the other hand, was hip—and he knew it. He was darting back and forth in his snowboard boots like he was wearing runners; comfort and traction weren't a concern. He carried all of the necessary equipment—his board—with ease under one arm as he waved and boasted of the day's adventures. He wore a small backpack that probably contained his lunch—and cell phone.

Know

- the characteristics of a comparison
- the rules for forming comparatives and superlatives
- letters and patterns that make the sound of **k**

Be Able To

- write a comparison
- identify the subject, predicate, and direct and indirect object in a sentence
- use apostrophes correctly

It's a myth that snowboarding is more dangerous than skiing for any particular age group. There are no statistics to support it. However, there *are* many advantages to learning to ski prior to snowboarding. The skills involved in edging, stopping and traversing are all quite similar to those of snowboarding and are easily transferred. There are also the issues of terrain awareness, safety and on-hill etiquette. It's important to learn the perils of ice, to deal with flats and steeps, and navigate through congestion—and it's easier to do that on skis. Also it's easier to learn how to get on and off lifts on skis, and skiing is less physically demanding than snowboarding when first starting out.

Almost every ski school in Canada now offers snowboard lessons, but be careful, they aren't all the same. Programs for snowboarders should be specialized, in the same way that ski lessons are. Look for a snowboard school with a proven program. Snowboarding should always be a fun experience, especially learning how.

Checkpoint: Comparison

Discuss how these characteristics of a comparison apply to the model. Later, you can use the list to help you revise your own work.

- ✓ It is based on direct observation, analysis, or research.
- ✓ The objects or ideas being compared must have some features in common, as well as some differences.
- ✓ It often begins with a discussion of one of the items being compared, then moves to a discussion of the other item, and concludes with a comparison of the two.

1. As a class, brainstorm possible topics for comparing two people, places, actions, or things. You might want to try one of the following topics:

   - two fictional characters
   - two authors
   - two books, TV shows, or films
   - two schools
   - two towns
   - two sports

2. Choose a topic (either from the brainstorm list or of your own choosing) for which you can gather at least some of the information by observation.

3. Make a Venn Diagram like the one below. Under A, list information about the first item being compared. Under B, list information about the second item being compared. Under C, list features that both items have in common.

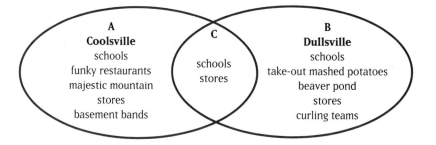

4. Write your comparison, using information from A in your first paragraph, information from B in your second paragraph, and information from C in the concluding paragraph. You should complete your writing with a concluding comment.

5. Refer back to the Checkpoint and revise your writing until you are satisfied with its focus, content, and organization. If possible, bring in photos or pictures of the things you are comparing to show members of your group. Then share your comparison with your group for their feedback.

Techno Tip

It's often helpful to accompany comparisons with charts or tables. Many word-processing programs allow you to make pie charts and graphs with the click of a mouse. Check out your program for details.

GRAMMAR

Be Able To

- identify the subject, predicate, and direct and indirect object in a sentence

The **simple subject** of a sentence is the noun or pronoun that tells who or what the sentence is about.

The **simple predicate** of a sentence is the main verb (one or more words) that tells what the subject is or does.

The most basic sentences are made up of a simple subject and a simple predicate. In the following sentences, the simple subject is in bold, and the simple predicate is in italics.

Johanna *skis.*   **Skates** *glide.*   **Children** *play.*

However, some verbs require more than just a subject to complete their meaning. For example, in the sentence *He wore a backpack*, the word *backpack* completes the meaning of the sentence. Without it, the rest of the sentence would not make sense. Words that complete the meaning of a verb in this way are called **objects.**

A **direct object** is a noun or pronoun that receives the action of an action verb. Direct objects answer the questions *what* or *who*.

simple subject	simple predicate	direct object
He	carried	all of the necessary equipment.

1. Identify the simple subject, simple predicate, and direct object in each of the following sentences.

   a) He clutched his skis.
   b) I spotted two boys.
   c) She lost her snowboard.

An **indirect object** is a noun or pronoun that comes before a direct object. Indirect objects answer the questions *to whom* or *for whom*.

simple subject	simple predicate	indirect object	direct object
She	offered	the kids	skiing lessons.

2. Identify the simple subject, simple predicate, and direct and indirect objects in the following sentences.

   a) He brought the girls their skis.
   b) Linda showed Sarah her snowboard.
   c) The instructor gave them a free lesson.

3. Write three sentences of your own that contain a direct and indirect object.

The **complete subject** of the sentence includes the simple subject along with any of its modifiers. The **complete predicate** includes the simple predicate along with any of its objects or modifiers.

complete subject | complete predicate

Almost every ski <u>school</u> in Canada | <u>offers</u> snowboard lessons.

simple subject | simple predicate

4. Copy the following sentences in your notebook and draw a vertical line between the subject and the predicate. Underline the simple subject and simple predicate, and write DO above any direct objects, and IO above any indirect objects. (Note: Not all sentences have objects.)

   a) He was darting back and forth in his snowboard boots.
   b) I never fully appreciated the popularity of snowboarding with kids.
   c) Lessons will give them a good grounding in the basics.
   d) In his one-piece, Barney-purple ski suit, he clutched his skis and poles in a desperate attempt not to drop them.

MECHANICS

Language Link

1. In the comparison between skiing and snowboarding, apostrophes are used in several places to show contractions. List four examples of this use of apostrophes from the model. Then find one other use of apostrophes in the model.

2. Comparing is a good way to understand concepts or ideas. Compare the pairs of sentences below, and for each pair write a rule that explains when an apostrophe is used.

   a) How many 7's are there in 1777.77?
      How many sevens are there in 1777.77?
   b) The grade seven class of '99 was going on a trip.
      The grade seven class of ninety-nine was going on a trip.

3. Look through several pieces of your writing to check your use of apostrophes. Have you used any apostrophes where they were not needed? Have you omitted apostrophes that should be there? Analyze your mistakes, and write a reminder in your notebook to help you avoid making the same mistakes in future.

Be Able To
- use apostrophes correctly

For more on the use of apostrophes in possessives, see Unit 3.

USAGE & STYLE

Language Link

Know
- the rules for forming comparatives and superlatives

Sentences may also contain various types of modifiers (adjectives and adverbs). Modifiers have three different forms for making comparisons:

Positive	Comparative	Superlative
cold	colder	coldest
demanding	more demanding	most demanding

Most **short modifiers** form comparisons by adding *-er* or *-est*. **Longer modifiers** are formed by using *more* (or *less*) or *most* (or *least*) with the positive form.

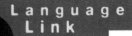

Irregular modifiers (such as *good, bad, well,* or *little*) don't follow any rules, so you just have to learn their comparative and superlative forms.

You will probably have no problem figuring out the comparative or superlative forms of most modifiers. However, there are a couple of common usage errors that you should be aware of.

> Never use **more** (or **less**) with an **-er** ending, or **most** (or **least**) with an **-est** ending. This forms a double comparison.

Bicycles are ~~more~~ better than cars, because they don't cause pollution.

British Columbia is the most beautiful~~est~~ province.

> Words like **different** and **unique** have no comparative or superlative.

A thing cannot be more or less different; it is either different or it is not different. Ditto for unique.

Quebec is ~~more~~ different from other provinces because more than half the population is French-speaking.

~~Kiwis' looks and taste make them the most unique fruit in the world.~~
Kiwis are unique among fruit both for their looks and for their taste.

> Use **few, fewer,** or **fewest** for things that can be counted; use **little, less,** or **least** for quantities that cannot be counted.

There are **fewer students** in the other class.

Her ski boots were **less comfortable** than her snowboard boots.

1. Rewrite the following passage in your notebook, correcting any errors in the use of comparative modifiers.

   In my opinion, dogs are more cool than cats. Dogs are the most unique of all pets because of the loyalty they show to their owners. Cats are less likelier to jump off the couch and meet you at the door with their tails wagging. While both pets sometimes enjoy lying on your lap, cats' claws feel sharplier than dogs. While cats require littler care, dog owners are more healthier than cat owners because they have to walk their pets. And cats can do less tricks than dogs.

2. Check through the draft of your comparison to make sure you have not made any of the modifier mistakes listed in this lesson. Correct any errors you find.

SPELLING

In words where you hear a **k** sound, chances are the sound is made by the letter **k** or patterns such as **nk, lk,** or **ke**. In some cases, however, the sound can be made by **c, ck,** or **qu**.

 Words to Watch For

These words, taken from the comparison at the beginning of the unit, all have a **k** sound.

buckle	backpack	etiquette	athletic	dynamic
traction	statistics	gymnastics	physical	unique

In your notebook, make a list of 8-10 words that make the sound of **k**. You can use words from this box, the comparison piece, and your personal reading. To help you learn the words, underline letters or patterns that make the sound of **k**.

1. Fill in the missing letters to complete **Words to Watch For**. Write them in your notebook.

   a) _ t _ _ _ _ _ e   b) _ _ n _ _ i _   c) _ _ _ c _ _ _ _   d) _ _ a _ _ _ _ _ _

2. Use the **Words to Watch For** to complete these sentences. Write the words in your notebook.

   a) Broken legs are sometimes put in _____.
   b) _____ show that you are much safer when you use safety gear.
   c) It's important to learn on-hill _____ .

3. **Words to Watch For** includes two pairs of words whose last syllables are spelled the same. What are they? Using words from your list and other words with the **k** sound, create at least two rhyming pairs. Use these words to create a poem that rhymes. Read your poem aloud to a group or the class.

Scroll Back

Edit and proofread your comparison, paying particular attention to the following:
- ❑ Have you used apostrophes correctly?
- ❑ Have you used the correct comparative or superlative form of any modifiers?
- ❑ Have you spelled all words correctly, especially those with the **k** sound?

Unit 7 Travelogue

What is a travelogue?

A travelogue is a description of a trip or a portrait of a place, usually as seen through the eyes of a visitor. The following travelogue, written by Brian Payton, is entitled "Surf City, CDA."

WHEN WE FIRST PULLED INTO the parking lot at the north end of Long Beach, I could scarcely believe my eyes. The wide, sandy beach stretched out before us beyond the limits of imagination. The lush green rain forest crowded the surrounding hills, and Lovekin Rock, awash in blue sky and sea, squatted just offshore. And there, right out in front of us in the rising swell, were the promised surfers. It was all true.

The day before, in the musty confines of the sports rental room at the University of Victoria, I had found myself staring incredulously at a giant surfboard sticking out from behind the hockey nets, tents, and canoes. The guy in charge confirmed the tantalizing rumour: up the coast of Vancouver Island, where the temperate rain forest meets the uninterrupted Pacific swell, there was surfing in the Great White North. This I had to see. I enlisted a friend, packed the board, and headed up-island.

When we arrived, we got out of our little red Rabbit, hopscotched across a mass of driftwood, and landed squarely on the sand of Long Beach. We took off our shirts. The warm spring sun and the sound of the tumbling breakers worked their hypnotic effect. Eventually, I pulled on an ill-fitting divesuit, picked up that ancient surfboard, and strode toward the sea. Before that moment, I had never been out past a shore break, let alone on top of a board. But as I felt the waves wash up around my ankles, I knew this was the start of an enduring affair.

Over the dozen years since that sun-drenched afternoon, I have been

Know

- the characteristics of a travelogue
- the rules for subject-verb agreement
- the patterns that make short vowel sounds

Be Able To

- write a travelogue
- use verbs effectively
- use commas with appositives

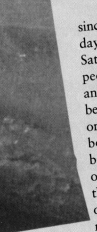

returning to Long Beach, watching it grow to become Canada's surfing capital. For those who have difficulty seeing the words Canada and surfing together, it may be a surprise to learn that surfers have been spotted in these waters since the 1960s. These days, on any summer Saturday, as many as 50 people—men, women, and children alike—can be seen out in the water on short boards, long boards, and body boards, with many others walking along the area's 10 kilometres of exceptional uninterrupted sandy shores.

People interact with Long Beach in countless ways. They explore the teeming tidal pools, observe the springtime parade of passing whales, or just hold hands and watch the sun go down on Canada. For me, it all comes back to the waves. I am happiest sitting on my board out past the breakers on an incoming tide, picking and choosing the best of the swells rolling my way. I like the idea of hitching a ride with a natural force that takes its cues from the circling moon and gathering storm. I relish the thought that my wave has travelled thousands of kilometres and brushed past whales, sharks, and salmon before finishing its journey with me riding its crest. In reality, of course, I wipe out and get tossed in the foam like a sock in a washing machine.

Checkpoint: Travelogue

Discuss how these general character-istics of a travelogue apply to the model. Later, you can use the list to help you revise your own work.

- ✓ It describes a place that the author has visited personally, and may include pictures.
- ✓ It describes events in the order in which they happened.

- ✓ It focuses on aspects of the trip or location that will be of particular interest to readers.
- ✓ Sometimes the place and the people are described generally; at other times specific places or individuals may be described in great detail.

1. Think about a trip you have been on recently. The trip may have been to another place within your neighbourhood or community, to a vacation area, or to some location in another province or country.

2. Decide who your audience will be. Adults? Children? Your peers?

Idea File
You could write a travelogue of an imaginary trip to your home town, for an audience of aliens....

3. Think about what aspects of your trip would seem most interesting or appealing to members of your audience. Consider including any or all of the following information:

- why you went there
- how you got there
- a brief history of the place
- your general impression of the place
- a description of the people you met
- cultural attractions and places of interest
- accommodations
- your feelings
- a comparison to other places

Arrange these details in chronological or another suitable order.

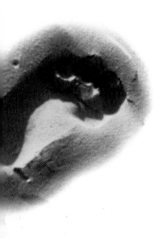

4. Write a first draft of your travelogue. Then refer back to the Checkpoint and revise your work until you are satisfied with its focus, content, and organization.

GRAMMAR

Know
- the rules for subject-verb agreement

When a word refers to one thing, it is **singular.** When it refers to more than one thing, it is **plural.** When we refer to the "number" of a word, we are referring to it as singular or plural.

> A verb must agree in number with its subject.

If the subject is singular, the verb must be singular. If the subject is plural, the verb must be plural. You will usually have no trouble figuring out what verb form to use. However, pay attention to the following examples, which show some of the trickier aspects of making subjects and verbs agree.

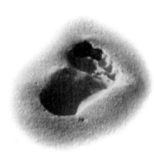

singular subject   singular verb

<u>Everybody</u> around here <u>loves</u> to surf.

Indefinite pronouns like *each, everybody, anyone,* etc. take singular verbs.

singular subject   singular verb

<u>Each of the students</u>   <u>has brought</u> a surfboard.

Each, not *students,* is the simple subject.

singular subject   singular verb

<u>Gymnastics</u>   <u>helps</u> you to balance on your surfboard.

Some words that look plural, like *gymnastics, mathematics,* etc., are actually singular.

plural subject   plural verb

<u>Mario and Lisa</u>   <u>are going</u> to Long Beach this weekend.

If the subject contains two or more words connected by *and,* use a plural verb.

Unit **7** **Travelogue**

singular subject   singular verb

<u>Fish and chips</u>   <u>is</u> my favourite meal when I'm at the beach!

When words joined by *and* form a single unit, use a singular verb.

singular subject   singular verb

<u>Either Mario or Lisa</u>   <u>is going</u> to Long Beach this weekend.

If the subject contains words like *either/or, not only/but also,* or *whether/or,* then the verb agrees with the part of the subject closest to the verb.

Techno Tip

You can use a grammar-check program to help you find subject-verb agreement errors when you do your writing on a computer. However, it's always a good idea to look through your writing yourself. Computers are not foolproof.

1. Rewrite the following sentences, correcting any errors in subject-verb agreement. Be prepared to explain your answer.

   a) The beach are an incredible place to spend my time.
   b) The cars and the bus is leaving at noon.
   c) This bunch of bananas cost ninety-eight cents.
   d) One of these girls are going to be chosen for the honour.
   e) This roll and butter taste good.

2. Write a paragraph describing a fictional trip to the beach. (Be creative! It doesn't have to be a *real* beach....) Include as many *mistakes* in pronoun-antecedent agreement as you can. Then exchange your paragraph with your partner's, and correct the errors.

3. Check through two or three writing assignments you have recently completed, looking for errors in subject-verb agreement. Which types of errors are you most likely to make? Think of a way to help you remember the rules you have trouble with.

A Challenge

The words *some, none, most, more, any,* and *all* can be singular or plural, depending on the context. (For example, *Some* of the water **was** in my mouth, *Some* of the waves **were** high.) Develop a rule that explains when to use a singular or a plural verb with these subjects. Present your rule to the class.

MECHANICS

Be Able To

- use commas with appositives

An **appositive** is a word or phrase that renames or explains a noun.

Appositives usually come immediately after the noun they rename or explain. They are set off from the rest of the sentence by commas.

appositive

Long Beach, <u>a stretch of land on the coast of Vancouver Island,</u> is a surfer's paradise.

appositive

Surfing, <u>or riding the waves,</u> is also very popular in California.

1. Write sentences using each of the following phrases as appositives. Make sure you punctuate each appositive correctly.

   a) my favourite place to relax
   b) the place where I live
   c) my best friend
   d) a river in my province

Strategy

You can use appositives to join short, choppy sentences into longer sentences that will make your writing flow more smoothly.

2. Combine each of the following sentences by making the second sentence into an appositive. Check the punctuation of your sentences.

   a) Brian Payton has been visiting Long Beach for 12 years. He is the author of "Surf City, CDA."
   b) Long Beach is on B.C.'s west coast. It is the surfing capital of Canada.
   c) For many years, people have been congregating at Long Beach with their surfboards. In fact, they have been doing so since the 1960s.

3. Check through a piece of descriptive writing you have completed, and consider combining sentences to form appositives—if you think doing so will improve the flow of your writing.

USAGE & STYLE

Be Able To

- use effective verbs

Good writers choose their verbs carefully so that their readers will get a clearer picture of what is happening. When you edit your work, look for verbs that are flat and uninteresting. Replace them (especially in descriptive writing) with words that make the character or setting come to life.

Ineffective:	The church **stood** on a hill above the town.
Better:	The church **towered** (or **loomed**) over the town.

Ineffective:	The bell **rang.**
Better:	The bell **chimed** (or **clanged,** or **tolled**).

1. Each of the sentences below has the verbs in **bold** print. For each verb, write more colourful verbs that might have been used instead.

   As I **walked** along the seashore, the waves **made** by the wind **hit** the rocks continuously. Birds **flew** overhead. Small children **ran** in and out of the water, and **made** sand castles with their hands. Surfers **found** big waves and **moved** their boards toward the shore. They **went** as fast as they could.

2. Reread the travelogue you wrote at the beginning of this unit, or another piece of writing you have completed recently. Check the verbs you used to see if they could be improved.

SPELLING

Know

- the patterns that make short vowel sounds

In this unit you will review the short vowel sounds of **a, e, i, o,** and **u.**

short a	short e	short i	short o	short u
pack	trek	trip	clock, walk	rush

From the chart above, you can see that the short **o** sound can be made by the letter **a** *(walk)* as well as the letter **o**. Short vowel sounds can also be made by combinations of vowels. In the word *dangerous,* for example, the **ou** combination makes the short **u** sound.

Words to Watch For

These words, taken from the travelogue at the beginning of the unit, contain examples of short vowel sounds.

tantalizing	temperate	imagination	offshore	musty
capital	exceptional	incredulously	hypnotic	tumbling

In your notebook, make a list of 8-10 words that have at least one short vowel sound and that can be difficult to spell. You can use words from this box, the travelogue, and your personal reading.

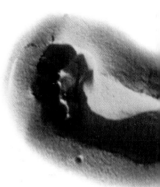

1. Use a **breve** (˘) to mark the short vowel sounds in each word in your list (for example, *schĕdule*). Use a dictionary if you need help.

2. In your notebook, create a short-vowel chart like the one on the previous page. How many words can you think of that contain a two-vowel pattern that makes a single short vowel sound? Work in a group to add these words to your chart. What symbol could you use to indicate the short vowel combinations?

3. Use your list words to write word analogy puzzles. (An **analogy** is a comparison that is based on a similarity between two things.) Here is an example:

   Small is to *little* as *outstanding* is to _____.
   (**Answer:** exceptional)

   Write the puzzles on one side of a blank page, and the answers on the other side. Exchange pages with a classmate and try to solve one another's puzzles.

Scroll Back

Edit and proofread your travelogue, paying particular attention to the following:

- ❏ Do all verbs agree with their subjects?
- ❏ Have you used commas to set off any appositives?
- ❏ Have you used strong, effective verbs whenever possible?
- ❏ Have you spelled all words correctly? Pay special attention to those words that contain two-vowel patterns that make a short vowel sound.

Unit **7** **Travelogue**

Unit **8** Descriptive Poetry

What is descriptive poetry?

A descriptive poem often focuses on one particular thing. It might be an ordinary, everyday sort of thing, or it might be something odd, unusual, or dramatic. But whatever the subject may be, poetry can transform or intensify the way we see it.

Poets strengthen their descriptions by using techniques such as alliteration, simile, and metaphor. These techniques help the reader gain strong sense impressions of the poet's subject. So we might not only "see" it; we may hear, touch, smell, and feel it too.

THE SHARK

He seemed to know the harbour,
So leisurely he swam;
His fin,
Like a piece of sheet iron,
Three-cornered,
And with knife-edge,
Stirred not a bubble
As it moved
With its base-line on the water.

Know

- the characteristics of descriptive poetry
- the function of adjectives
- how punctuation can enhance a poem's meaning
- how vowels can be influenced by **r**

Be Able To

- write a descriptive poem
- identify alliteration and similes
- spell words containing **r**-controlled vowels

His body was tubular
And tapered
And smoke-blue,
And as he passed the wharf
He turned,
And snapped at a flat-fish
That was dead and floating.
And I saw the flash of a white throat,
And a double row of white teeth,
And eyes of metallic grey,
Hard and narrow and slit.

Then out of the harbour,
With that three-cornered fin
Shearing without a bubble the water
Lithely,
Leisurely,
He swam—
That strange fish,
Tubular, tapered, smoke-blue,
Part vulture, part wolf,
Part neither—for his blood was cold.

— E. J. Pratt

WRITER'S WORKSHOP

Checkpoint: Descriptive Poetry

Discuss how these general characteristics of a descriptive poem apply to the model. Later, you can use the list to help you revise your own work.

✓ It often uses techniques such as alliteration, simile, and metaphor to create strong sense impressions or to describe emotions.

✓ Each word is chosen with care for its sound, rhythm, and meaning.

✓ It does not always follow traditional rules of punctuation and capitalization.

1. Decide on the topic for a descriptive poem. Choose something (or someone) that you know well, or feel strongly about. Or you might want to write about something that has sparked your interest or fired your imagination.

Idea File

Here are a few ideas to get you thinking:

person: an interesting-looking stranger whom you always see on the bus

place: an unfamiliar street that suddenly reminds you of an incident from your childhood

thing: an old shirt lying on the sidewalk (but a block away it looked like something else)

2. Decide on a poetry form. You could use "The Shark" as your model, or you might wish to read other poems until you find a pattern you prefer. (Consider writing your poem as a haiku, a cinquain, or a shape poem, for instance.)

3. Write the following words in your notebook: FEEL, HEAR, SMELL, TASTE, and SEE. After each word, write words to describe your person, place, or thing.

4. As you write your poem, refer back to the words you wrote in #3. Give your poem a title.

5. Refer back to the Checkpoint and revise your poem until you are satisfied with its focus, content, and organization.

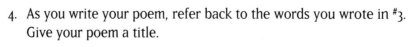

Adjectives are words that modify a noun or pronoun.

Adjectives are used in sentences to describe *(enormous, rainy)*, to show how many *(21)*, to point out *(this, that, these, those)*, and to show how much *(less, some, more, part)*.

Possessive adjectives (more often called possessive pronouns) tell who owns something.

His, her, their, my, our, and *your* are possessive adjectives.

The words *the, a,* and *an* are special adjectives called **articles.**

The shark had **an** alarming habit of slicing through water without making **a** bubble.

1. Based on the sentence above, write a rule for the correct use of *a* and *an.*

2. Look at the poem "The Shark." Find the following:

   a) five examples of adjectives that describe
   b) one example of an adjective that shows how many
   c) two examples of adjectives that point out
   d) one example of an adjective that shows how much
   e) one example of a possessive adjective
   f) one example of an article

3. Look at the poem you wrote in the Writer's Workshop. List all the adjectives you used in the poem, and classify them according to the uses and types of adjectives listed above.

A Challenge

Choose one of the adjectives from "The Shark," and list as many synonyms as possible for that adjective. Why do you think the author chose to use the word he did?

Unit **8** Descriptive Poetry

4. You have probably seen poems that are written so that the words form a shape on the page. Choose a thing or person, and write a shape poem made up of adjectives that describe what you chose. (Use fresh, vivid adjectives to make your poem more compelling.) The shape of the poem should relate somehow to its subject. (For example, if you have decided to write about a truly strange vase that you saw at a friend's house, the poem could be in the shape of that vase.)

MECHANICS

Know

- how punctuation can enhance a poem's meaning

There are no specific rules for punctuation when writing poetry. Some poets often put punctuation at the end of some or all of the lines, while others write without any punctuation at all.

1. Look at the poem at the beginning of this unit. What punctuation was used? In each case, explain why you think the poet punctuated the poem the way he did.

2. In groups of three, look at other examples of poems in a poetry anthology. Choose one of the poems your group liked. Rewrite the poem on a large piece of chart paper, using a bright colour for the punctuation marks. Read the poem aloud to the class. After the reading, discuss the poet's use of punctuation.

USAGE & STYLE

Be Able To

- identify alliteration and simile

Poets paint pictures with words, in the same way painters do with colour and shape. And just as painters use different techniques to create different effects, so poets have at their disposal a number of different types of language techniques. These are known as **figurative language**. In "The Shark," two of these methods stand out: alliteration and simile.

Alliteration is the repetition of the same initial consonant sound in words close to one another.

> **L**ithely,
>
> **L**eisurely,
>
> He swam—

1. Alliteration can help create a particular feeling. What feeling or mood do you think E. J. Pratt wanted to create with his repetition of the letter **L** in the lines above? How else does his choice of words add to that effect?

2. Write three descriptive poems (or parts of poems), each just three lines long. At least two of the three lines in each poem should begin with the same letter. Make your descriptions as vivid as you can. Choose each poem's letter carefully: the sound of it will affect the mood of the poem!

A **simile** compares two things using the words *like* or *as*.

> His fin,
>
> Like a piece of sheet iron,

3. This time, write three poems (or parts of poems) that are *two* lines long. The second line of each poem should begin with *like* or *as*. (Even though you have only two lines to work with, make your description as compelling as possible.)

4. Find five words, phrases, or lines from the poem "The Shark" that clearly paint pictures in your mind. With a partner, discuss why you think these words, phrases, or lines are so effective.

5. Listen to the lyrics of some of your favourite songs, and identify four examples of simile or alliteration that you think are effective. With your teacher's permission, play the songs, or recite the lyrics for the class, identifying the use of simile or alliteration and explaining what it adds to the song.

6. Review the poem you wrote in the Writer's Workshop, and consider whether you could add any figurative language to your description.

Metaphor—
another form
of figurative
language—
is discussed
in Unit 14.

Unit **8** Descriptive Poetry

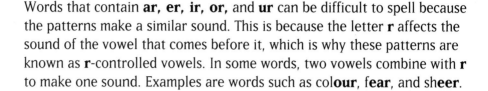

SPELLING

Know

- how vowels can be influenced by **r**

Be Able To

- spell words containing **r**-controlled vowels

Words that contain **ar, er, ir, or,** and **ur** can be difficult to spell because the patterns make a similar sound. This is because the letter **r** affects the sound of the vowel that comes before it, which is why these patterns are known as **r**-controlled vowels. In some words, two vowels combine with **r** to make one sound. Examples are words such as col**our**, f**ear**, and sh**eer**.

Words to Watch For

All of these words contain at least one **r**-controlled vowel sound. Most have been taken from the poem at the beginning of the unit, and the rest are words you will encounter and use frequently.

harbour	tapered	cornered	neither	conquer
tubular	shearing	harden	navigator	surrender

In your notebook, make a list of 8-10 words that contain an **r**-controlled vowel sound and that can be difficult to spell. You can use words from this box, the poem, or your personal reading. To help you learn the words, underline the letters that make the **r**-controlled vowel sound in each word.

1. On a blank page, write each word from your list, leaving blanks where the **r**-controlled vowel sounds occur. (Use the same number of blanks as there are vowels.) Exchange lists with a partner and fill in the blanks.

2. Is it tubul**er** or tubul**ar**? Navigat**or** or navigat**er**? It's easy to misspell words that end with **ar, er,** and **or,** especially when the word is one you don't use very often. Work with a partner for five minutes to brainstorm as many of these words as you can. Each of you should write down each word quickly, without worrying about the spelling. After the brainstorming is complete, compare your lists. Look up in a dictionary words that you're unsure of.

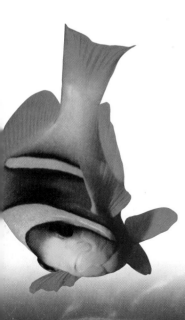

Strategy

Here are two ways you can learn to spell words that end in **ar, er,** or **or**:

- Write a word two ways if you are not sure of its spelling. Look at the words and choose the one that looks right. It probably is correct.
- For particularly difficult words, think up a mnemonic device, such as "tornado navigator." (The **or** in *tornado* helps with the **or** in *navigator.)*

3. Choose one word from your list. Develop a mnemonic device that will help you remember the word's spelling.

4. Illustrate the mnemonic device you created in question 3. Post it where others can see it. Can they identify the word you chose to illustrate?

Scroll Back

Edit and proofread your poem, paying particular attention to the following checklist:

❏ Have you used vivid, lively, appropriate adjectives?
❏ Have you used punctuation to add meaning or emphasis to your poem?
❏ Have you used figurative language to create strong images or comparisons?
❏ Have you spelled all words correctly, particularly those with **r**-controlled vowels?

Present It!

Prepare a reading of your poem for your classmates. What sound effects, lighting, props, or dramatic effects can you use to enliven your presentation?

Unit **8** Descriptive Poetry

Exposition

Expository writing surrounds us. Car repair manuals, self-help books, basketball rule guides, recipes—any writing that communicates facts is exposition. It's writing that tells who, what, when, where, why, and how. If you've ever been frustrated by poorly written instructions, you'll know that good expository writing involves more than simply presenting facts. It's crucial that these facts be organized in order to meet the needs of the reader.

This section contains four forms of expository writing: factual account, instructions and procedures, report, and explanation. Although these forms differ from one another, each presents factual information about a process, idea, or event in a format that's useful and understandable to the reader.

Features of Exposition

- Exposition involves presenting or summarizing facts.

- Expository writers must decide what facts to present and how much detail to include based on how the information will be used by the reader.

- Expository writers try to choose words and images that make information easy for their audience to understand.

- The writer's personal opinions and value judgments aren't usually part of expository writing. When they are included, they're clearly identified as opinions, not facts, and are backed up by evidence.

What is a factual account?

A factual account is the retelling of an event. It focuses on presenting the facts in the order in which they happened. The ability to recount events accurately is important in many disciplines, from mathematics (explaining how you arrived at a solution) to journalism (newspaper articles often recount events). The following account, written by Daniel Cohen, is entitled "The Flying Bomb."

The giant silvery airship turned to make its final approach. Two hundred feet over the field its powerful engines growled into reverse. The ship stopped and hovered motionless. Lines were dropped to the ground. The ground party rushed to pick them up.

That is how the giant zeppelin Hindenburg came into Lakehurst, New Jersey, on the evening of May 6, 1937. Its arrival had been delayed for nearly ten hours by bad weather. But the weather had cleared, and the approach looked smooth and natural.

The Hindenburg had flown all the way from Germany. The trip had taken seventy-seven hours. Aboard were a total of ninety-seven passengers and crewmen.

The Hindenburg was the fastest and most luxurious way to cross the Atlantic Ocean in 1937. It had already made ten crossings without a single mishap.

The giant zeppelin was still a novelty. Its arrival always made news. Among those waiting on the ground for the arrival were many photographers and radio men. One of the radio men was Herb Morrison of Station WLS. He was describing the moment for his listeners. He told them how gracefully the great silver ship glided in. Then suddenly his voice registered shock. "It's burst into flames!" he shouted into the microphone. "Oh my . . . it's burning, bursting into flames . . . Oh, the humanity and all the passengers." The radio announcer's voice broke into sobs. He couldn't go on.

Know

- the characteristics of a factual account
- the various ways that adverbs are used
- a variety of transition words
- the sound made by the patterns **al, el,** and **le**

Be Able To

- write a factual account
- use commas with adverbs
- spell some words that contain the **al, el,** and **le** patterns

THE EVENING STAR

That is how many people first learned that the Hindenburg had exploded and burned. Within less than forty seconds the entire ship was ablaze. People on the ground were stunned for a moment. Then they began to run for their lives, as the flaming giant crashed toward them. In a few terrible seconds thirty-five people had died as a result of the tragedy. Others were horribly burned or badly injured trying to jump to the ground. Remarkably, more than half of those aboard survived the disaster.

As a result of the Hindenburg explosion and fire zeppelin travel was completely abandoned. All remaining passenger-carrying zeppelins were grounded, permanently . . . .

Just exactly what caused the Hindenburg explosion no one knows. No one may ever know. Both the United States and Germany conducted investigations. Everybody who might possibly know anything about the explosion was interviewed. The official conclusions were that some sort of electrical spark had set off the explosion. No one could agree what caused the spark.

There were a lot of unofficial rumours as well. Some said that a bomb had caused the explosion. The Germans had been afraid of a bomb. Before the Hindenburg left Germany, all the passengers and crew had been searched carefully. The entire zeppelin was examined from top to bottom. No bomb was found. Still, two German air force officers rode along on the trip as a special precaution.

There are many theories about who might have planted a bomb and why. In 1937 Germany was firmly in the control of Adolf Hitler's Nazi party. There were a lot of people who had good reason to hate the Nazis.

The bomb theory is still discussed today. But no one has ever been able to find any solid evidence to support it. So the question of exactly what caused the Hindenburg explosion remains open.

* * *

WRITER'S WORKSHOP

Checkpoint: Factual Account

Discuss how these characteristics of a factual account apply to the model. Later, you can use the list to help you revise your own work.

✓ The purpose of a factual account is to recount an event.

✓ It often begins by answering the 5 W's (who, what, when, where, and why).

✓ Details of the event are usually presented in chronological order.

✓ It may conclude with a personal reaction, a look at why the event happened, or a justification for actions taken by someone involved with the event.

1. Think of an event that has happened recently at your school or in your community.

Idea File

You might choose to write a factual account of a sports event that you or your school was involved in, a project undertaken by a group within the school, recent changes to the school environment, a performance you attended, or a field trip.

2. Use an outline like the one below to map out your account. Copy the chart into your notebook, and fill in the blanks with facts about your topic.

Topic
Background (who, what, when, where, and why)
Details (in chronological order)
Personal Reaction/Explanation/Justification

3. Using your plan, present your factual account orally to a classmate. Ask your classmate if your account was clear, and if it included enough details. Based on his or her comments and your own judgment, write a first draft.

4. Refer back to the Checkpoint and revise your work until you are satisfied with its focus, content, and organization.

GRAMMAR

Know
- the various ways that adverbs are used

Adverbs can modify verbs, adverbs, and adjectives.

adverb modifying the verb *made*

It had <u>already</u> made ten crossings without a single mishap.

Just as nouns have modifiers (known as adjectives), so a verb or adjective may have modifiers. These are called adverbs. Many, but not all, words that end in **-ly** are adverbs.

Adverbs can be very useful when you are recounting a series of events. They can be used to tell **how** (*quietly, carefully*), **when** (*soon, then*), **where** (*here, there*), and **to what extent or degree** (*completely, partly*). Use them to clarify the sequence of events, to specify a location where events took place, or just generally to make your account more precise.

Adverbs can even be used to modify another adverb.

Some thought that a bomb had **most** likely caused the explosion.

In the example above, the adverb *most* modifies the adverb *likely.*

Strategy
Before you use an adverb to modify a verb, ask yourself if there is a more precise word that could replace both the adverb and the verb. For example, instead of saying *ran quickly*, you could say *raced.* Instead of saying *cried loudly*, you could say *wailed.*

Unit **9** Factual Account

1. Look at "The Flying Bomb." Find the following examples of adverbs.

   a) three examples that tell how
   b) one example that tells when
   c) two examples that tell where
   d) one example that tells to what extent or degree

2. Write the following headings at the top of a page in your notebook: HOW, WHEN, WHERE, and EXTENT/DEGREE. Write each of the following adverbs under the correct heading.

very	then	quite	finally
secretly	there	sorrowfully	here
underground	too	quickly	afterwards
later	ready	extremely	hurriedly

A Challenge

Tom Swifties are puns using adverbs ending in *-ly* (for example, *"Pass the vinegar," he said sourly*). Complete each of the following Tom Swifties, either on your own or in small groups.

"I love these cookies," she said _____.
"Where is the sun?" he asked _____.
"I'll find that mutt," the owner said _____.

Now try writing two Tom Swifties of your own. Share them with the class.

MECHANICS

Be Able To
- use commas with adverbs

Often adverbs stand out in sentences. They seem to modify the whole statement. Look at the following sentences from the model.

Remarkably, more than half of those aboard survived the disaster.

All remaining passenger-carrying zeppelins were grounded, **permanently.**

So, the question of exactly what caused the Hindenburg explosion remains open.

Notice how the adverbs in these sentences are set off from the rest of the sentence with a comma. This is not always the case, but it is done frequently, depending on the emphasis and the rhythm the writer wants.

1. With a partner, read the following sentences aloud with and without the commas and discuss what effect the comma has on the emphasis placed on the adverb.

   a) **Obviously,** people were upset by the explosion.
   b) **Unfortunately,** there were not many survivors.
   c) Some of the passengers survived, **amazingly.**
   d) Nothing, **however,** could be found to prove what had happened.

2. Working with a partner or alone, develop six sentences using commas to set off the adverb for emphasis. (Write sentences that sound as though they were taken from a very dramatic factual account.) Develop two sentences each with the adverb placed in the following positions.

   a) beginning of the sentence
   b) end of the sentence
   c) somewhere in the middle of the sentence

   Read your sentences to another pair of students. At the end of each sentence, have them identify the adverb emphasized. Reverse roles and do the same.

USAGE & STYLE

When you write a factual account, try to link one event to the next smoothly. In order to avoid using the word *then* too frequently, writers often use **transition words** at the beginning of sentences. These words show the passing of time and the sequence of events. Listed below are some useful transition words.

Know
• a variety of transition words

See Unit 13 for transition words that help to build a convincing argument.

a few minutes later	first	so
about that time	furthermore	soon
after a while	in addition	suddenly
also	last	then
as a result	meanwhile	therefore
but	next	when
during the next	second	while
finally	similarly	within

Unit **9** Factual Account

1. Examine the beginnings of the sentences in the model. Identify five transition words that have been used in the factual account. Write these in your notebook.

2. Compose five sentences of your own, using each of the transition words from question 1 as the beginning of a different sentence. Be creative! Write sentences that could be part of an exciting (and imaginary) factual account.

3. Examine your own factual account. Have you used a good assortment of transition words?

A Challenge

Over the next week, look through newspapers, magazines, and books for other transition words. Add five to the list above.

Language Link

SPELLING

Know
- the sound made by the patterns **al, el,** and **le**

Be Able To
- spell some words that contain these patterns

Words that contain **al, el,** or **le** can be difficult to spell because the patterns can make a similar sound. This is because the letter **l,** like the letter **r,** can influence the sound of vowels that come before it (**al, el**), or after it (**le**). The letter **l** can have the same influence on two vowels that combine to make one sound (for example, **ia** in *official).*

 Words to Watch For

All of the words below contain the **al, el,** or **le** pattern. Some are taken directly from the factual account at the beginning of the unit, while the others are based on root words used in the account.

arrival	total	horrible	official	novel
natural	terrible	remarkable	electrical	survival

In your notebook, make a list of 8-10 words that end in **al, el,** or **le** and that can be difficult to spell. You can use words from this box, the factual account, and your personal reading. Underline the final letters in each word to help you remember the spelling.

Strategy

Some words can be difficult to spell because we can't rely on the sounds we hear. One way to learn these words is to practise writing them. Choose several words from your list. Print or write each word in different ways, changing the style, size, and colour.

1. Exchange your word list with a partner's. Write each of your partner's words, leaving blanks for the final two letters. Return the list to your partner, then fill in the missing letters in your own word list.

2. Write a synonym or antonym for six words from your list. Challenge a partner to match your synonyms and antonyms to your list words.

3. Seven words in the **Words to Watch For** can be transformed into adverbs by adding the suffix **-ly**. Write the seven words (as adverbs) in your notebook. What is tricky about adding the **-ly** suffix?

4. A factual account often begins with a colourful title to capture the reader's interest. Using words from your list, create titles for five different factual accounts. Give your titles to a partner and challenge him or her to write the introductory sentence for each account. The introductory sentence must include a word from your partner's list. Use your imagination to decide what each piece could be about! For example, a factual account entitled "Mall Survival" might begin, *My arrival at the mall was marked by a totally unexpected volcanic eruption.*

Scroll Back

Edit and proofread your account, paying particular attention to the following checklist:

❏ Have you replaced adverbs plus verbs with more precise verbs when possible?
❏ Have you used commas when appropriate with adverbs that modify whole sentences?
❏ Have you used transition words to move smoothly from one event to the next?
❏ Are all words spelled correctly? Pay special attention to words containing the **al, el,** and **le** patterns.

Unit 9 **Factual Account**

Unit ⑩ Instructions and Procedures

What are instructions and procedures?

Instructions and procedures explain how to make or do something, usually through a sequence of steps or actions. These may be in oral or written form. If you've ever had any concerns about how to pack a picnic basket, for example, the following procedures might help you out.

An Explanation for Everything

Picnicking Procedures

Packing a Picnic Basket

A properly maintained picnic basket can reduce the chance of hunger or thirst during a hike or outing. To increase the effectiveness of your picnic basket, follow these guidelines:

- Distribute items evenly on the floor of the basket, placing the heaviest items on the bottom (example: "tuna sandwich" on top; "bowling ball" on bottom).
- Never exceed the load limits of your basket. Overloading can result in seriously bruised fruit.
- Always secure the egg salad in a sealed air-tight container. (See Emissions Control.)

IMPORTANT: Be sure you know your picnic basket and how to use it safely. Remember, a picnic basket is NOT A TOY!

Sandwich Assembly

Assembling a sandwich requires special tools and access to condiments. Unless you have the equipment and expertise, consult a professional for assistance.

At the end of this unit you will

Know

- the features of instructions and procedures
- the correct use of colons
- when to drop the letter **e** or change **y** to **i** when adding suffixes

Be Able To

- write instructions or a procedure
- identify sentences according to their four purposes
- use verbs that accurately describe actions

How It All Works — An Explanation for Everything

1. Remove two slices of bread from bag.
2. Apply a light coat of your preferred condiment to slice A.
3. Place one (1) leaf of lettuce on slice A.
4. Position a piece of cheese on top of lettuce.
5. Insert cold cuts (or other foodstuff) between slice A and slice B.
6. Gently compress slice A and slice B.
7. Using a sharp instrument cut sandwich in half.
8. Seal sandwich in protective wrapping.

NOTICE *Do not leave your picnic basket unattended in the woods. This could result in a basket-snatching by a smarter-than-average bear.*

Protecting Your Picnic Basket

The ant (iridomomyrmex humilis) is the natural predator of the picnic basket. Ant invasion can result in a ruined picnic. So exercise extreme caution at all times.

WARNING

When you encounter an army of ants, move your picnic basket to an elevated area immediately.
(See Removable Picnic Table.)

97

WRITER'S WORKSHOP

Checkpoint: Instructions and Procedures

Discuss how these characteristics of instructions and procedures apply to the model. Later, you can use the list to help you revise your own work.

- ✓ Their purpose is to show the audience how to perform a set of actions.
- ✓ They may begin with a brief introduction, along with a list of necessary tools or ingredients.
- ✓ Steps in the process are often numbered.

- ✓ They are always written in the order in which the procedure is carried out. (Clear order is particularly important in this type of writing.)
- ✓ They are written in the imperative (as a series of commands).
- ✓ They often include illustrations or diagrams.

1. Decide on a procedure you wish to explain. Your instructions might be serious or silly (like the model). Also decide who your audience will be, and how familiar it is with your topic. As you write your instructions, make sure that the language level matches the needs of your readers.

Idea File

Having trouble thinking of a topic? How about writing instructions on how to make a mess; how to drive your brother/sister crazy; how to prepare a favourite food; how to eat a chocolate cookie; how to make friends on the Internet; how to design a Web page; how to fix a flat tire on a bike; how to program a VCR; how to tie your shoes....

2. List all the tools, instruments, ingredients, or parts needed to perform the task.

3. Write the steps in the procedure in a numbered list. Try to make each step short enough to be easy to remember, but not so short that your reader will get irritated. ("Make an omelette" is definitely too short.) If possible, perform the procedure as you write (but watch out for those greasy egg splatters!).

4. Add any diagrams that are necessary, and give your instructions a title that clearly indicates their purpose.

5. If possible, give the instructions to someone (preferably from your target audience) to try. Ask the person for feedback on what was unclear or confusing in your procedure. (If the person responds with "What's a frying pan?" you might want to ask someone else.) Use their comments and the Checkpoint to revise the focus, content, and organization of your instructions.

GRAMMAR

Language Link

Be Able To
- identify sentences according to their four purposes

Sentences can be categorized by their purposes. Read the following sentences:

> A properly maintained picnic basket can reduce the chance of hunger or thirst during a hike or outing.

> Do you now understand how to assemble a sandwich?

> Remove two slices of bread from bag.

> Remember, a picnic basket is NOT A TOY!

1. What is the purpose of each of these sentences? (Hint: What type of punctuation mark is used at the end of each one?)

A Challenge

Unscramble the following words to find the formal names of the sentences above. (Hint: In earlier grades you might have known these sentences as **statement, question, command,** and **exclamation** sentences.) Record the names in your notebook.

dlcitearvae	iverentogtair
ivitarepme	ertmlxcaaoy

2. Examine the following two sentences. Why is there a period at the end of each, instead of a question mark? In other words, what is the *purpose* of each of these sentences?

a) I wonder if my procedures will work.
b) I asked my brother to try out my procedures.

Unit 10 Instructions and Procedures

3. The sentences below each have a different purpose. Rewrite the sentences in your notebook, transforming each of them into the three *other* types of sentences. You might have to do some rewording. (For example, the sentence *Why am I following these instructions?* might become *Please tell me why I'm following these instructions, I wonder why I'm following these instructions,* and *I can't believe I'm following these instructions!*) Identify the purpose of each of your new sentences.

   a) Distribute items evenly in the basket.
   b) Assembling a sandwich requires special tools.
   c) Let's go bowling in the meadow!

Strategy

As a general rule, use direct commands as often as possible when writing instructions. Instead of *The vegetables should now be cooked,* write either *Cook the vegetables now* OR *Check the vegetables now to see if they are cooked.* Otherwise you may confuse your readers (and mess up their meals).

4. Look through your set of instructions and make sure you have used direct commands whenever necessary.

Language Link

MECHANICS

Know
· the rules for using colons

Colons are often used to introduce a list that follows a complete sentence.

The words that come before the colon must be able to stand on their own as a sentence.

Correct: Before you begin, assemble the following items: measuring spoons, a measuring cup, and one large mixing bowl.

Incorrect: Before you begin, assemble: measuring spoons, a measuring cup, and one large mixing bowl.

Objects are discussed in Unit 6.

The second example is incorrect because the verb *assemble* lacks an object *(the following items),* and so the words that come before the colon do not form a complete sentence.

1. Check the model to find one example of a colon that's used to introduce a list. Then find five other similar examples elsewhere in this textbook. Write the examples in your notebook.

Strategy
Colons are often preceded by the key words *following* or *these*.

2. Read the sentences below, and in your notebook correct any mistakes in the use of colons.

   a) Please pack: bread, lettuce, cheese, and cold cuts.
   b) My recipe consists of: flour, soda, sugar, eggs, sour milk, and butter.
   c) Follow the route by: reading the map, looking at signs, and asking for directions.

Colons are also used after the salutation in a business letter; in expressions of time written as numerals; and to introduce long or formal quotations.

Dear Ms. Bannerji: 6:15 a.m.   Rule 14A reads as follows:

3. Write a brief letter to someone. (Anyone!) Your letter should demonstrate all the rules for colons that were covered in this unit. (Try to make it as funny or as imaginative as you can.) After you have completed your letter, exchange it with a partner's and edit each other's work.

4. Check the procedures you wrote at the beginning of this unit. Did you use colons correctly?

USAGE & STYLE

Be Able To
- use verbs that accurately describe actions

Instructions are all about taking action. Since verbs are the action words in the sentence, it's important to use verbs that accurately describe what you want your reader to do.

1. Listed below are some action verbs used in recipes. Each has a specific meaning that can be important for the success of a recipe. Working in groups of four, add 10 other action verbs that are often found in recipes.

   cut   chop   dice   purée   boil   bake

Unit **10** Instructions and Procedures

2. Each of the first five steps in "Sandwich Assembly" begins with a verb. Write the first five steps of another procedure. (The procedure can be an actual one, or it can come entirely from your imagination.) Begin each step with a different action verb.

3. Create a glossary of 10 action verbs for other types of instructions or procedures. Illustrate five of these verbs. List each verb in boldface (if you are using a computer), then write a short definition. (It can be serious or silly.) Here's an example:

> **saw** To pass the mean-looking end of a saw vigorously back and forth over something you want to cut off.

A Challenge
Some instructions are written entirely with diagrams. Try explaining how to put something together, or make something, using only diagrams.

4. Look back at the action verbs you used in your instructions. Do they accurately describe what you want your reader to do? Revise any verbs that you think could be improved.

Language Link

SPELLING

Know

- when to drop the letter **e** or change **y** to **i** when adding suffixes

Adding suffixes to words that end in **e** or **y** can be tricky, but there are some basic rules that can make spelling these words easier. You'll discover many of these rules in the following lesson.

Words to Watch For

All of these words contain a suffix. Some are taken directly from the instructions at the beginning of the unit, while the others are based on root words used in the model.

reduction	removable	distributor	heaviest	enduring
bruised	annoyance	exercising	immediately	effectiveness

In your notebook, make a list of 8-10 words that have a root word ending in **e** or **y** and that have a suffix. You can use words from this box, the instructions, and your personal reading.

Strategy

You can follow these rules when spelling words with suffixes.

- In a word with a long vowel sound, drop the **e** when adding a suffix that starts with a vowel (for example, *note + able = notable*).
- In a word that ends in **y**, change **y** to **i** when adding a suffix that does not begin with a vowel (for example, *fancy + ful = fanciful*).

1. Write the **Words to Watch For** that are examples of these rules. When you are finished, write the root of each of the words.

2. Reread the strategy for this lesson. If you drop the **e** when adding a suffix that starts with a vowel, what do you do when adding a suffix that starts with a consonant? Work with a partner to write a rule, then find four examples.

3. If you change **y** to **i** when adding a suffix that begins with a consonant, what do you do when a suffix begins with a vowel? Work with a partner to write a rule, then find four examples.

4. Make a summary of rules that help you add suffixes to words that end in **e** or **y**. For each, write two examples. Place the summary in your Personal Dictionary so that you can refer to it easily.

5. Use words from your list to create advertising slogans for three different products. For an added challenge, include an instruction in each slogan. For example, *Tunes for Toning: Put the "sing" back into exercising!* You might design a billboard advertisement featuring one of your slogans and an appropriate graphic.

Scroll Back

Edit and proofread your instructions carefully, paying particular attention to the following:

- ❏ Have you used direct commands when appropriate?
- ❏ Have you used colons correctly?
- ❏ Have you used accurate action verbs?
- ❏ Are all words spelled correctly? Pay special attention to those with suffixes added to words that end in **e** or **y**.

Unit (11) Report

What is a report?

Reports are factual texts that present information clearly and concisely. Research reports are prepared by people in many occupations. The following report is taken from H. I. Peeple's book entitled *Bubble Gum*.

It's a *marble*... it's a *balloon*... it's a BUBBLE!

The biggest bubble-gum bubble ever blown was twenty-two inches around! You've probably blown some good-sized ones yourself, but could you blow one that large? And have you ever wondered where those chewy blobs known as bubble gum come from?

Before there was bubble gum, there was chewing gum. And the story of chewing gum begins thousands of years ago, when cavepeople chewed wads of tree sap.

Since then, practically everyone has found something to chew, including the ancient Greeks, the Mayan Aboriginals, and many others. Indians in New England gave the first American colonists a tangy spruce sap to chew. Later colonists chewed wax.

The gum we chew today had its beginnings in 1869. An unpopular Mexican commander fled from Mexico to Staten Island, New York. He brought with him a chunk of chicle, a milky-white gummy substance. He wanted to sell the chicle, which he thought could be made into rubber.

Inventors couldn't make rubber out of the chicle. However, one inventor named Thomas Adams discovered that chicle was better to chew than spruce gum or wax. He added the dried root bark of a sassafras tree for taste. Around 1871, he took his invention to a local drugstore, where two gumballs were then sold for a penny. The first modern chewing gum was on the market!

Know

- the stages in writing a report
- the function of prepositions
- when (and when not) to use quotation marks with particular words
- the sound made by schwa vowels and how they are represented in the dictionary

Be Able To

- write a report
- use the prepositions *in/into* and *on/onto* correctly

Bubble gum was discovered on August 8, 1928, by Walter Diemar. He had been experimenting for months with different mixes and was surprised when he blew an enormous bubble. The only food coloring he had was pink, so the first bubble gum was pink. Today, bubble gum comes in all colors, but most of it is still pink.

Originally, bubble gum had only one flavor. Today, cinnamon, spearmint, licorice, strawberry, and peppermint are only a few of the many flavors to choose from. What's your favorite flavor?

Exactly how bubble gum is made is kept a secret, but we do know the basic process. First, the gum base is ground up and heated. Then it is dried. Next, it is cooked in large kettles until it is as thick as maple syrup. The cooking sterilizes the gum base.

The cooked gum base is put into huge mixing vats, and all the other ingredients are added to it. Sugar sweetens the gum. Corn syrup also sweetens gum and keeps it fresh.

Softeners, such as vegetable oils, help blend the ingredients and keep the gum soft and moist.

All these ingredients are mixed together, and the gum is kneaded like bread dough and flattened into sheets. Machines cut the sheets into sticks, gumballs, pellets, or chunks. Finally, the different pieces are covered with powdered sugar to prevent sticking.

Once the gum is cut into shapes, other machines wrap the pieces in aluminum foil or paper to keep them fresh and juicy. Then the gum is gathered and sealed in airtight packages. The packages are labeled with the date and the ingredients.

What do you think happened when that twenty-two-inch bubble, the world's biggest, popped? It probably covered the entire head of the person who blew it! What do you think she did? She probably tried again. Because there's no end to the number of bubbles you can blow with one wad of bubble gum!

Checkpoint: Report

Discuss how these characteristics of a report apply to the model. Later, you can use the list to help you revise your own work.

✓ Its purpose is to present or summarize relevant information about a topic.

✓ The introduction catches the reader's interest and tells what the report is about; the body provides key information, arranged by topic; and the conclusion summarizes the main points, and relates back to the introduction.

✓ Reports are usually written in the third person *(it, he, she)*, and in present tense.

1. Make a *More About ...* book with your partner. Begin by brainstorming a list of everyday items that you could find out about. Possible topics might include toothpaste, breakfast cereal, paper, pens, or ice cream. Find a partner, and pick a topic to report on.

2. Make a KWL chart like the one below for your topic, and fill in the first two columns.

What do I already **Know**?	What do I **Want** to find out?	What did I **Learn**?
• gum has different flavours	• how is gum made?	

3. Think of possible sources of information about your topic and make a list of key resources you will consult for information. Some possibilities include

nonfiction books	newspapers	CD-ROMs
almanacs	periodicals	Internet
atlases	dictionaries	audio-visual media
magazines	people	encyclopedias

4. As you search through your resources, record answers to the questions in the second column of your chart in point form, recording only key words or phrases. In addition, you may want to add other information that you think your audience will find interesting.

5. Arrange the information in a logical order and write a draft.

6. Refer back to the Checkpoint and revise your report until you are satisfied with its focus, content, and organization. Then fill in the third column of the KWL chart, explaining what you learned by doing your report. You may also wish to add other information about "The Most Interesting Part" or "The Best Part."

GRAMMAR

Know
- the function of prepositions

A **preposition** is a word (or group of words) that shows how a noun or pronoun is related to another word in the sentence.

He brought **with** him a chunk **of** chicle.

The preposition *with* links the verb *brought* to the pronoun *him;* the preposition *of* links the noun *chunk* to the noun *chicle.*

Prepositions come before nouns or pronouns. Here are some common, single-word prepositions:

about	among	between	like	over	under
above	around	down	near	past	until
across	as	during	off	since	up
after	before	in	on	through	upon
against	below	inside	onto	to	with
along	beneath	into	outside	toward	without

There are also **compound** and **group prepositions,** such as *across from, ahead of, in front of,* and *owing to.*

1. Find five examples of prepositions in the model. In each case, identify the two words that are linked by the preposition.

Unit **11** Report

2. The paragraph below has had the prepositions removed from it. In your notebook, write prepositions that might have been used in each of the spaces in the paragraph. What does the absence of the prepositions tell you about their importance in sentences?

> Chewing bubble gum has its pros and cons. _____ the person doing the chewing, there is the delicious flavour _____ the gum and the pleasure _____ blowing bubbles. _____ _____, chewing gum provides exercise _____ your face muscles. However, there is also a negative side to this activity. The appearance _____ someone chewing gum, and creating huge amounts _____ noise while doing it, can be distasteful. This is why, _____ course, teachers often do not allow students to chew gum _____ school hours.

3. Examine the report you wrote in this unit and make a list of the prepositions you used. Then divide your list into three groups: those that show time relationships *(before, until)*, those that show place relationships *(above, across)*, and those that show *manner* of relationship (these include *for, like, of, with,* and *without).*

4. Design an ad campaign for "Preposition Appreciation Day" with the aim of promoting awareness of and appreciation for prepositions(!).

MECHANICS

Know

- when (and when not) to use quotation marks with particular words

Sometimes, when you are writing reports, you may have to explain the meaning or origins of a particular word.

> "Chicle" is the coagulated milky juice of the sapodilla tree used as the main ingredient of chewing gum.

When you set a word apart in a sentence in order to define it, place quotation marks around it (or use italics).

1. Where necessary, place quotation marks around the words that are discussed in the following statements. Write the words in quotations in your notebook.

a) The noun bubble means airball, globule, or blister, while the verb bubble means to boil, percolate, foam, fizz, fizzle, sparkle, or gurgle.

b) Where do you think the word cinnamon comes from?

Strategy

Many writers use quotation marks around words they are unsure of (for example, *Blowing bubbles in class is an "egregious" activity*), or when using expressions that they are afraid may not be appropriate to the context *(The Queen "split" right after the royal reception)*. Remember, only use quotation marks when you are defining a term. If you don't feel you can include a word or expression without enclosing it in quotation marks, then change your choice of language.

2. Rewrite the following passage, removing any unnecessary quotation marks.

Ice-cream sundaes were "invented" in the 1890s. Ice-cream sodas had been popular for several decades, but many people considered it "immoral" to drink soda on Sunday. So owners of soda fountains invented a "treat" that had no soda in it: the sundae. The name "sundae" was probably used to avoid offending churchgoers, and perhaps to persuade people that they could be eaten on "any day" of the week.

USAGE & STYLE

Be Able To
- use the prepositions *in/into* and *on/onto* correctly

The prepositions **in** and **on** are usually used to indicate position; the prepositions **into** and **onto** usually indicate movement.

1. Draw pictures (stick figures are fine) to illustrate the difference between the following sentences.

The gum is pulled on the conveyor belt.
The gum is pulled onto the conveyor belt.

2. Use the correct preposition in each of the sentences below.

a) I shoved a wad of gum *(in, into)* my mouth.
b) I put my chewing gum *(in, into)* the left pocket of my jacket.
c) The bubble burst just as the teacher walked *(in, into)* the room.
d) Gum was stuck *(in, into)* my hair and all over my face.
e) The pack of gum was *(on, onto)* the floor.
f) I pulled the gum out of my mouth and stuck it *(on, onto)* the desk

SPELLING

Know

- the sound made by schwa vowels and how they are represented in the dictionary

Say the word **bubble** out loud. Listen to how the stress is placed on the first syllable—**bub**—and not on the second syllable—**ble**. When a vowel sound occurs in an unstressed syllable, it is often pronounced with a neutral "uh" sound, and is called a **schwa** vowel. The schwa vowel sound is represented by the symbol ə: **bŭb′ əl**. Any vowel—**a, e, i, o, u**—can make the schwa sound "uh." Words that contain this sound can be difficult to spell because the sound doesn't belong to one vowel.

Words to Watch For

These words, taken from the report at the beginning of the unit, contain schwa vowels.

marble	colonists	substance	discovered	kneaded
wondered	practically	inventory	ingredients	flavour

In your notebook, make a list of 8-10 words that have at least one schwa vowel sound and that can be difficult to spell. Use a dictionary to confirm that the words you choose do have a schwa. You can use words from this box, the report, and your personal reading.

1. Choose five words from your list. Write the words with their syllable breaks. Add the symbols that show whether vowels are long or short. Add stress marks to show which syllables are stressed, and circle the syllables that contain a schwa vowel. Check your work by looking up each word in a dictionary.

Strategy

Link patterns in words you are learning to spell to patterns in words you already know how to spell. For example, knowing how to spell *marble* can help you spell *proba***ble**.

2. Match the syllables below to make four words. Write the words in your notebook. (Hint: Look to **Words to Watch For** for help.)

nĭsts   ĭn   mŏr′ kol′   ə   stəns dē   əns sŭb′ bəl grē′

Create a syllable scramble using the pronunciations of four words from your own list. Challenge a partner to solve your scramble.

3. In your notebook write the **Words to Watch For** that match these definitions.

   a) past-tense verb; a synonym for *found*
   b) noun; a synonym for *early settlers*
   c) past-tense verb with a silent consonant
   d) noun; it is small and round

4. Copy these marks and symbols in your notebook. Now, imagine that you have to explain them to someone who has never used a dictionary. Write a brief explanation of each mark, including an example to help your reader understand. (For example, *The* ē *symbol represents a* **long e.** *This is the vowel sound heard in the word "need." The sound can be made by the vowel patterns* **ea, ee, ei, ie, y,** *and* **ey.***)*

   a) ′ (primary stress)   b) ′ (secondary stress)   c) ă (short a)

   d) *n* (noun)   e) ə (schwa vowel)   f) ī (long i)

Scroll Back

Edit and proofread your report, paying particular attention to the following:

❏ Have you used quotation marks to indicate a word that is being defined?
❏ Have you avoided using quotation marks to justify inappropriate words?
❏ Have you used *in, into, on,* and *onto* correctly?
❏ Have you spelled all words correctly, especially those containing schwa vowels?

Present It!
Write your report on a computer. Print out a copy, design a cover, and prepare a table of contents. Then present your report to the resource centre for other students to use as a reference.

Unit (12) Explanation

What is an explanation?

An explanation usually provides information on *how* something works (for example, how a tornado whirls so alarmingly) or *why* something happens (for example, why your heart starts to pound when you're afraid). Some explanations throw light on both how *and* why, like this excerpt from an article by Patricia Gadsby entitled "Why Mosquitoes Suck."

You **know** a creature is in deep, deep trouble when people don't think twice about whacking it.

Even animal rights activists aren't so quick to leap to the mosquito's defence. The only good mosquito, many people would say, is not just dead but well and truly dead, reduced to a bit of insect juice on the wall.

Why do mosquitoes bug us this way? And why some of us so much? (*Why me?*)

Considering our bad attitude, it's a wonder mosquitoes even come near us—an insanely risky proposition from their viewpoint. That's probably why some mosquito species figured long ago they'd rather tuck into an unconscious host, an unmovable feast as it were, and voted by and large to nip at night. The nipping's done with a proboscis, a sort of springy syringe with a hollow needle formed by interlocking mouthparts and an outer sheath that rides up when the needle slides through your skin and probes for blood.

But hitting the sweet spot isn't so easy—ask any intern drawing blood from a patient for the first time. Or ask José Ribeiro, a medical entomologist at the National Institute of Allergy and Infectious Diseases, who will gladly give you the gory details. "Less than 5 percent of skin is blood vessel, so the mosquito has to fish. It casts its proboscis back and forth under your skin, sawing through tissue and probing an area ten seconds at a time." After several such "search castings" and no luck, the insect withdraws completely and tries another patch of skin. But if it gets a good probe into one of your

At the end of this unit you will

Know

- the characteristics of an explanation
- when to use commas with a series of prepositional phrases
- common blends and the sounds they produce

Be Able To

- write an explanation
- identify and write prepositional phrases
- explain any necessary jargon and technical language

small blood vessels, it freezes and sucks from the hemorrhage, pumping in little spitballs of vessel dilators and blood thinners to keep its meal running freely. (An allergic reaction to mosquito drool is what produces those itchy red lumps, if you've wondered.) A mosquito can suck two to three times its weight in blood, no trouble. That's tantamount to a 150-pound human vacuuming up 300 to 450 pounds of food.

At this point, stretch receptors in the mosquito's hugely bloated abdomen, sensing imminent blowout, initiate an urgent message to the brain, saying in effect, "Whoa there, skeeter—pull out!" Marc Klowden, an entomologist at the University of Idaho, has videos showing what happens when you prevent the signal from the abdominal receptors from reaching the brain: too much is never enough for these mosquitoes, and they eat until they explode.

Even under normal circumstances, once a mosquito has eaten its fill, "it's so heavy it can barely fly," according to Ribeiro. Stuporous and swollen as a blimp, it looks for a place to lie low and do what anyone would do after going on the mother of binges—it excretes like crazy. After a few hours the mosquito has reduced its blood meal by half into a super-nutritious slush.

Thankfully, at any given time, in any population, less than half the mosquitoes are biters. That's because, first, only females are hematophagous (Greek for "blood eaters"). Males are sweet nectar-loving types, peacefully sipping at nature's juice bar. Second, most females feed on blood only when they need the extra protein to finish making the eggs; for routine fuel they'll use plant sugars, too. In fact, feeding on blood seems a pretty well-orchestrated event, dangerous enough that females have built-in controls to switch it on and off—they don't seek out victims more than they have to. Remind yourself of this the next time you're being eaten alive. Things could be worse.

WRITER'S WORKSHOP

Checkpoint: Explanation

Discuss how these characteristics of an explanation apply to the model. Later, you can use the list to help you revise your own work.

✓ Its purpose is to illustrate a cause-and-effect relationship.

✓ It often begins with a question or statement (*why, how*) and then goes on to provide an answer or supply details.

✓ Stages, steps, or parts are carefully described and linked to one another.

✓ The level of detail and use of technical terms depends on the expertise of the audience.

1. Working in groups of four, write HOW TO ... at the top left-hand side of a piece of paper, and WHY ... on the top right-hand side. Brainstorm possible topics under each heading. Individually, choose one of the topics to write about and identify an audience for your explanation.

2. Gather facts to explain your topic. Some possible sources for your facts are textbooks, encyclopedias, Web searches, science centres, or people (interviews).

3. Using the data you have collected, organize your information. For example, if the topic of your explanation is "Why Tornadoes Occur," you might organize your information in terms of cause and effect:

Causes	Effect
tornadoes	1. clashing warm and cold air masses
	2. high humidity
	3. high winds that begin to rise

4. Write a first draft. Use cue words such as *if… then, because, as a result, so, since,* and *therefore* to signal to your reader that you are providing a cause-and-effect explanation.

5. Refer back to the Checkpoint and revise your report until you are satisfied with its focus, content, and organization.

GRAMMAR

A **prepositional phrase** is a group of words that begins with a preposition, ends with a noun or pronoun, and may include modifiers of that noun or pronoun.

Prepositional phrases function as a single unit in the sentence. Almost all prepositional phrases function as adjectives or adverbs.

modifies *casts*

It casts its proboscis back and forth <u>under your skin</u>, sawing <u>through tissue</u> and probing an area ten seconds at a time.

modifies *sawing*

The noun or pronoun in a prepositional phrase is called the **object of the preposition.**

Preposition	Modifier	Object
under	your	skin
through	—	tissue

I. In your notebook, identify the objects of the prepositions in each of the following sentences, and indicate whether each phrase acts as an adjective or an adverb.

a) I was badly bitten during the night.
b) With bleary eyes, I raised a rolled-up newspaper.
c) Every time I turned the light out, this pesky mosquito would whine around my ear.
d) Finally, I just hid my head under the hot, heavy blanket.
e) All night I dreamed that a mosquito of giant proportions was chasing me.
f) Mosquitoes are the bane of my existence.

Strategy

Whenever possible, choose the simplest way of expressing what you want to say. While prepositional phrases are often necessary, be on the lookout for instances where a single modifier would do the same job.

2. In your notebook, replace each of the prepositional phrases below with an adjective placed in front of the noun.

a) all cities in Canada
b) dates of importance
c) the road in the country
d) the shingles on the roof

A Challenge

One of the longest place names in the world is Llanfairpwllgwyngyllgogorychwyrndrobwllllantysiliogogogoch, which translates as "St. Mary's Church by the pool of the white hazel trees, near the rapid whirlpool, by the red cave of the Church of St. Tysilio." Your local town council wants to rename your home town or city and get it into the *Guinness Book of World Records*. Compose a new name to describe your city or town that contains even more prepositional phrases than the Welsh town above!

3. Write 10 prepositional phrases (for example, *in the evening* or *from Regina*) on small strips of paper. Have a partner write five short sentences (for example, *The lobster crawled* or *The teapot leaked*) on five more small strips. Then take turns adding the prepositional phrases to the sentences to create nonsense sentences. Use the phrases as both adjectives and adverbs.

Language Link

MECHANICS

Know

- when to use commas with a series of prepositional phrases

In Unit 5 you learned that commas are used to set off items in a series. Sometimes in your writing you have more than one prepositional phrase in a row. When this is the case, you need to set off the phrases with a comma.

During the evening, before the storm, everything was quiet.

1. Rewrite the following sentences, inserting a comma, where necessary, between the prepositional phrases.

   a) Without a whisper without a sound the mosquito flew towards its prey.

   b) The woman swatted at the mosquito left and right up and down without once making contact.

   c) The bullying bug flipped into the air around in a circle and landed on her wrist with a very small smile.

   d) She tossed the swatter through the door over the fence and into the pond.

   e) Put the swatter in the kitchen beside the bug spray and sledgehammer.

USAGE & STYLE

Language
Link

Be Able To
- explain any necessary jargon and technical language

To make your explanation clear to your audience, avoid using technical terms whenever possible. **Jargon** is language that is familiar to people in a particular field, but may not be familiar to those outside that field. When you must use such terms, make sure you explain them in language your audience will understand. The examples below show how the author of "Why Mosquitoes Suck" explained the technical terms *proboscis* and *hematophagous*.

> The nipping's done with a proboscis, a sort of springy syringe with a hollow needle formed by interlocking mouthparts and an outer sheath that rides up when the needle slides through your skin and probes for blood.

> That's because, first, only females are hematophagous (Greek for "blood eaters").

1. Write any words or terms in the model explanation that you do not understand. Look for an explanation in a dictionary. Then rewrite the sentences, either explaining the term in the text or substituting a term you think is more easily understood.

2. Choose one of the computer terms listed below, and explain to a partner what it means. Your partner should pretend that he or she is new to computers, and try to imagine what questions such a newcomer might have. Then reverse roles and try another computer term.

interface   boot up   log on   hard drive   input   virtual reality

SPELLING

Know

- common blends and the sounds they produce

In a blend, such as **pr, sp,** or **str,** you can hear the sounds of each individual consonant. Often, however, when you say a blend you glide over the second (or third) letter. Correcting your pronunciation of a blend can help you spell it correctly.

Words to Watch For

Each of these words, taken from the explanation at the beginning of the unit, contains a blend.

| creature | species | feast | springy | withdraws |
| host | proposition | completely | slush | built |

In your notebook, make a list of 8-10 words that contain a blend and that can be difficult to spell. You can use words from this box, the explanation, and your personal reading. To help you learn the words, underline the blend in each word.

1. Make rhyming word families for two lesson words. Choose the words, then write rhyming words. There is one condition: your rhyming words must include the blend.

Strategy

When spelling a challenging word that contains a blend, try spelling the word aloud. Say each letter clearly (including letters in the blend), then write the word.

2. Use the **Words to Watch For** to complete these sentences.
   Write them in your notebook.

   a) The _____ welcomed his guests for the evening.
   b) Some say that humans are an odd _____.
   c) The _____ was too good to refuse.
   d) The dinner party was _____ ruined by those mosquitoes!

3. In your notebook, write the word that does **not** belong in each group.

   a) fear, feat, feast, feel
   b) snow, slush, windshield, rain
   c) creation, creature, creative, create
   d) withdraws, advances, moves forward

4. The word *proboscis* comes from the Greek word *proboskis.* In this
   word **pro** is a prefix, meaning "before" or "in front of." *Boskis* is from
   the verb *boskein,* which means "to feed." Find four examples of words
   where **pro** is used as a prefix. Write a history for each word. (Hint: Use
   a dictionary for your research.)

Scroll Back

Edit and proofread your explanation, paying particular attention
to the following:

❏ Have you replaced prepositional phrases with single adjectives where
   appropriate?
❏ Have you used commas to separate prepositional phrases in a series?
❏ Have you avoided the use of technical terms and jargon whenever
   possible, and explained any terms that your audience will not
   understand?
❏ Are all words spelled correctly, including those that contain blends?

Unit **12** **Explanation**

Persuasion

Persuasive writing is writing that gets things done—that moves readers to believe or to act. Whether you're trying to persuade government officials to clean up an environmental hazard, or simply to convince a friend that one James Bond film is superior to all other James Bond films, persuasive writing is a way to let people know what you think and to encourage others to support your views.

This section contains four forms of persuasive writing: opinion piece, advertisement, review, and persuasive letter. By carefully gathering evidence to support their causes, the authors of these pieces demonstrate how to use persuasion to achieve a variety of goals.

Features of Persuasion

- Persuasive writing aims to move the reader to support a point of view or to act in support of an idea or cause.

- A persuasive piece often begins with a description of the topic or issue and a statement of the author's point of view or position.

- The main part (or body) of the piece often presents arguments and evidence in favour of the author's position, arranged in the most convincing order.

- The piece may conclude with a call to action or a recommendation.

What is an opinion piece?

An opinion piece is usually found in magazines, newspapers, and journals. The subject of an opinion piece is usually a current issue of public concern. The writer expresses an opinion about the issue with the intention of persuading readers to support his or her viewpoint. See if *you* are persuaded by the following opinion piece, which appeared in a Guelph, Ontario newspaper called *The Speed River Current*.

The So-Called Teenage Problem

by Tristan Zimmerman

SKATEBOARDING IS STEREOTYPICALLY viewed as a pastime for trouble-making teens, and it is often associated with violent rap music, property damage, and loss of business for downtown store owners. But in the eyes of these so-called "hoodlums," skateboarding is not a criminal sport but rather an acrobatic challenge, involving speed, skill, and strength.

Every sport provides exercise and fun, although most involve taking risks. As skateboarding involves its own hazards to both skaters and bystanders, it is justly unsuitable for our downtown core. Picture a baseball game being played during a sidewalk sale—the results would be disastrous. That is why we have ballparks.

This is precisely the argument between skaters and the community. We know we deface curbs with wax, and mark benches. So why downtown? Because skateboarding is a communal sport, a culture in itself, and downtown is a suitable meeting place for skaters city-wide. We don't enjoy the unfriendly attention from the police—in fact, we hate it. We now face the risk of receiving a first offender's fine of $50.

Know

- the characteristics of an opinion piece
- when to use parentheses
- the diphthongs made by the patterns **ou, ow, oi,** and **oy**

Be Able To

- write an opinion piece
- identify sentence fragments and correct them
- use transition words to help build a convincing argument

Today, with skateboarding such a popular sport among youth (approx. 300+ skaters in the Guelph area), we need a place to enjoy it.

At least as long as I have been skate-boarding, city officials have been talking about building a skate-park, but when asked to go through with it they state they are incapable due to a lack of funding. Come on! The money accumulated from skate-boarding fines alone in the last few years would be enough to build at least two well-equipped skate-parks in our community.

We aren't asking for much: a paved surface with a few ramps.

A skate-park would effectively cut down on the presence of skaters in the downtown core, as skate-parks in Kitchener have proven. We aren't asking for much: a paved surface with a few ramps. So if you skateboard, have friends or children who do, or are someone who feels intimidated whenever a crowd of skateboarders pass by, please call or write your city councillor and show your support for building a skate-park in Guelph.

WRITER'S WORKSHOP

Checkpoint: Opinion Piece

Discuss how these characteristics of an opinion piece apply to the model. Later, you can use the list to help you revise your own work.

✓ It aims to convince an audience to accept a point of view or take a particular action.

✓ The introduction usually states the opinion being defended.

✓ Arguments in the body are arranged in an effective order, from least important to most important, for example.

✓ The argument is supported by facts and figures, examples, or incidents rather than generalizations and feelings.

✓ The conclusion may restate the opinion, or call readers to action in support of a proposition.

1. Select an issue that you feel strongly about and write a sentence that clearly states your opinion on the topic. It could be an issue relating to school, home, your community, or the world. Here are a few pr to get you thinking.

   - _____ would make things better for me.
   - If we _____, our home/team/school/community would improve.
   - I believe there is a better solution to the problem of _____.

2. Decide what group or individual you need to convince in order to realize your purpose. Direct your arguments to that audience.

3. Collect ideas or arguments in a web like the one below. Choose the arguments that you think would be most convincing to your audience, and list facts to back up each argument. (If you don't have any facts, find some!)

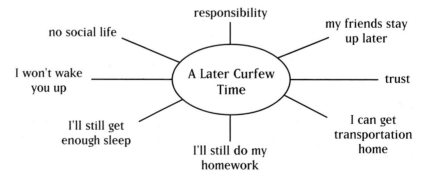

responsibility

no social life

my friends stay up later

I won't wake you up

A Later Curfew Time

trust

I'll still get enough sleep

I can get transportation home

I'll still do my homework

4. List your arguments in order, from weakest to strongest.

5. Write a draft. As you write, think about your audience. Will they be convinced by these arguments? Is your writing style appropriate? If your audience includes friends or family members you can keep your language fairly informal. If you are directing your writing at members of the community, or a school or company official, you will want to write in a more formal style.

6. Refer to the Checkpoint and revise your draft until you are satisfied with its focus, content, and organization.

Formal and informal styles are discussed in Units 4 and 14.

GRAMMAR

Language Link

A **sentence fragment** is an incomplete sentence. Either the subject or the verb (or both) is missing, so the sentence expresses only part of a thought.

Be Able To
- identify sentence fragments and correct them

We won't give up. **Not ever.**

We need to fight to keep our school, **Even if it means going to court.**

I'm here to talk about my pet peeve. **Noisy eaters.**

1. Explain why the second sentence in each example below is a sentence fragment. Then rewrite it as a complete sentence.

   a) Some people think skateboarders are dangerous to people. Such as pedestrians.
   b) Recreation is important. In cities too.
   c) We know we deface curbs with wax and mark benches. And sidewalks.
   d) We need space. Whenever we go skateboarding.

2. Identify the sentence fragments in the following passage, and rewrite the paragraph correctly.

   A decision to build a skate-park would show sound judgment. Really. Teenagers must be given opportunities for leisure. Not hanging out. We could also provide demonstrations of our skills. Jumping, wheelies, and speed. A blast!

Unit **13** Opinion Piece

Idea File

Writers sometimes use fragments intentionally, in order to add force and drama to their writing. (For example, *We won't give up. Not ever* is more persuasive than *We won't ever give up.*) However, in formal writing, sentence fragments are usually not acceptable.

MECHANICS

Know

- when to use parentheses

Use parentheses around words that add information (or for short asides or afterthoughts), and that do not affect the structure of the sentence.

Today, with skateboarding such a popular sport among youth (approx. 300+ skaters in the Guelph area), we need a place to enjoy it.

1. What information has been added to the sentence above? Suggest another way the author could have included the information. Why do you think he chose to use parentheses?

Strategy

Dashes are covered in Unit 14.

Overuse of parentheses will make your writing disjointed. Ask yourself if the information you want to enclose in parentheses is really necessary. If not, cut it. If it is, consider making it part of a complete sentence, or try using a pair of dashes—like this—instead.

2. Each of the sentences below contains information that should be in parentheses. Rewrite each sentence in your notebook, inserting the parentheses.

a) My great-grandparents visited Kitchener previously known as Berlin many years ago.

b) Frequent accidents occurred at the track about 30 last year but this is no reason to close it.

c) It is my belief and the members of our club support me that a skateboarding park is imperative for this city.

d) According to the results of an informal survey I conducted the survey myself three out of four students think the cafeteria food is overpriced.

e) A Canadian, James Naismith 1861–1939, invented the game of basketball.

Techno Tip

It's easy to conduct a search for parentheses on your computer. When the Find function asks you to "Find What" just key in "(" and then read each entry to see if the parentheses you have used are necessary. (It's a good idea to do a search for the end parenthesis mark as well, to make sure you have always used them in pairs.)

USAGE & STYLE

Language Link

Be Able To
- use transition words to help build a convincing argument

Connecting arguments should build on each other and flow together. To accomplish this, authors use transition words or expressions to join one idea or sentence to the next. Look at the words in the list below.

all together	but	for example	meanwhile
also	even though	for instance	next
although	finally	however	so
at least	first	in addition to	then
because	furthermore	in the same way	therefore

1. Find three examples of transitions in the model.

2. Working in pairs, choose a controversial issue you both agree on (for example, year-round school, athletes' big salaries, or violence on television). Next, take turns making oral statements about the topic. After the first statement, begin each following statement with one of the transition words or phrases in the list above.

1st student: I agree with year-round schooling.

2nd student: **However,** the summer holiday should still be several weeks long.

1st student: **Furthermore,** those weeks should be in July.
etc.

See Unit 9 for transition words that show a sequence of events.

Unit **13** Opinion Piece

3. Reread your opinion piece and look for places where you could clarify or strengthen your argument by adding transition words or phrases such as those on the previous page.

SPELLING

Know

- the diphthongs made by the patterns **ou, ow, oi,** and **oy**

In a diphthong, the first vowel glides into the second vowel to make a new sound. The patterns **ou** and **ow** make one diphthong; the patterns **oi** and **oy** another. For example, listen to the vowel sound you hear in *loud* and *growl*, then the vowel sound you hear in *toil* and *toy*. Notice how in each pair of words the patterns sound the same. This paragraph contains three words that have diphthongs (in addition to the examples). Can you find them? (Two of the words are used more than once.)

 ### Words to Watch For

Some of these words have been taken from the opinion piece at the beginning of the unit. Others share a root with words in the opinion piece or have been added to represent words you might want to use when writing your own opinion piece. All contain a diphthong.

proudly	councillor	destroying	noisily	annoy
downtown	spoiled	enjoyable	uncrowded	foiled

In your notebook, make a list of 8-10 words that contain a diphthong and that can be difficult to spell. You can use words from this box, the opinion piece, and your personal reading. To help you learn the words, underline the pattern that makes the diphthong in each word.

1. Choose three **Words to Watch For**. Make rhyming word families for each word. Underline patterns that are the same in each word.

Strategy

One way to help remember a word's spelling is to find a word within a word. Say you have trouble spelling the word *spoiled*. It might help you to remember that the word *oil* can be found in *spoiled*. Make a simple sentence to remind you of the word's spelling; for example, *Too much oil spoiled the salad.*

2. Choose five words from your word list, and find a smaller word in each one. Make up simple sentences that you can use when you have to spell the words.

3. Find **Words to Watch For** that are synonyms or antonyms for these words.

   a) irritate   b) suburb   c) packed   d) quietly   e) building

4. The pattern **ough** can make different sounds, including the **ou** diphthong. Work with a partner to create a list of words with the **ough** pattern. Sort the words into categories, based on the sound **ough** makes. Did you identify an **ough** word that has the **ou** diphthong?

5. Work with a partner to make a list of root words that contain the **oi/oy** diphthongs. Examine the words in your list. Create a sentence to explain where in a word the diphthongs are usually found.

6. If you had to help someone learn to spell words that contain diphthongs, what advice would you give? List strategies that would help the person spell these words.

Scroll Back

Edit and proofread your opinion piece, paying particular attention to the following checklist:

- ❑ Have you avoided using sentence fragments?
- ❑ Have you limited your use of parentheses?
- ❑ Have you used transition words to strengthen your argument?
- ❑ Are all words spelled correctly, especially those that contain the diphthongs covered in this unit?

Unit 13 **Opinion Piece**

Unit (14) Advertisement

What is an advertisement?

Effective advertising catches your attention by direct, simply worded text and compelling visuals. It is usually meant to appeal to a specific audience. The following ad was taken from a brochure for Triumph motorcycles, and so contains more text than you would usually see in a magazine, newspaper, or billboard ad.

TRIUMPH

Performance and style to take your breath away.

The all-new T595 Daytona signals the dawn of a new era in Triumph's history—technology, looks and performance at the cutting edge of motorcycle design.

The 955cc fuel-injected three-cylinder motor is explosively fast, howling up to 10,700 rpm and generating a staggering 130PS (128hp) on the way. Yet it's mild and predictable when you're taking it easy.

The engine serves another purpose too, adding its own stiffness to that of the lightweight, aluminum trellis frame. The combination of this rigidity and the top quality, fully adjustable suspension has produced the most accurate, responsive handling of any Triumph yet, helped by the overall weight of just 198 kg (436 lbs).

The T595 Daytona doesn't just meet modern supersport standards, it moves them on.

Know

- the characteristics of an effective advertisement
- how to combine independent and subordinate clauses to form a sentence
- how a metaphor differs from a simile
- common homophones and their meanings

Be Able To

- write an effective advertisement
- use dashes effectively
- create metaphors
- distinguish between an independent and a subordinate clause

Sensational acceleration, exhilarating handling, intoxicating looks.

The bodywork is functional, of course—scything a path through the air to protect the rider, but it's also a masterpiece of style. Mouth-wateringly beautiful, elegantly British, and so well balanced you have to look again and again to take it all in. The blend of technology and exquisite looks even extends to the paint, with an ultra-gloss shine and shimmering multi-tone colour that finish the Daytona to perfection.

T595 Daytona—fast forward to the future.

Daytona T595

Checkpoint: Advertisement

Discuss how these characteristics of an advertisement apply to the model. Later, you can use the list to help you revise your own work.

✓ It is usually targeted at a specific audience.

✓ It often relies on a combination of headlines, words, and images to draw the reader's attention.

✓ It may use adjectives, adverbs, and figurative language to make the product appeal to the audience's emotions or desires.

✓ The vocabulary may also stress the practical benefits of the product.

1. As a class, brainstorm a list of possible products that could be used for an advertisement. Your items may be real or imaginary.

2. Working in pairs or on your own, choose one of the products suggested by the class, or select an item of your own. Decide who would be most likely to buy this product, and prepare a profile of your target audience, listing their age, gender, income range, interests, and educational level, along with any other characteristics you think are important.

3. Decide what features of your product will appeal most to your target audience. For each feature, ask yourself, "What desire or need of my target audience does this feature satisfy?"

Idea File

Ads often try to appeal to our desire to be popular, powerful, happy, successful, younger (or older), or more important.

4. Using what you have learned about your audience and your product, write an ad. Include pictures or photographs to make your ad more appealing. Think of a slogan or headline to grab the reader's attention.

5. Try your ad on a "consumer"—preferably someone from your target audience—and ask him or her for feedback. Did the ad attract his or her attention? Were the benefits of the product obvious? Was the ad convincing? Refer back to the Checkpoint and revise your ad until you are satisfied with its focus, content, and organization.

GRAMMAR

Language
Link

> A **clause** is a group of related words that has a subject and a predicate.

Every sentence contains at least one clause. An **independent clause** can stand alone as a complete sentence because it expresses a complete thought. A **subordinate clause** begins with a subordinating conjunction (e.g., *while, that, which, after, because*) and cannot stand alone because it does not express a complete thought. Subordinate clauses must be combined with independent clauses to make sentences.

Independent clause:	you will be fantastically popular
Sentence:	You will be fantastically popular.
Subordinate clause:	if you buy this toothpaste
Sentence:	You will be fantastically popular if you buy this toothpaste.

Idea File
The connecting words *and, but, or,* and *nor* are coordinating conjunctions. They join two *independent* clauses.

Conjunctions are discussed in Unit 4.

1. Identify two clauses in each of the following sentences, and tell whether they are independent or subordinate.

   a) The motor can be explosively fast, but it is also mild and predictable.
   b) When the sale ends, the price of these collectible motorcycles will go up.

2. Rewrite the following sentences in your notebook. In each sentence, underline the clauses and indicate their types.

   a) People who buy our product understand that quality comes first.
   b) Our toothpicks are the best because they are handpicked in the forests of Brazil.
   c) Try our salsa once and you will never try any other kind.
   d) When you need a lift, reach for Chocobits!

Unit **14** **Advertisement**

Know
- how to combine independent and subordinate clauses to form a sentence

Be Able To
- distinguish between an independent and a subordinate clause

3. Write three sentences of your own that have both an independent and subordinate clause. Exchange your sentences with a classmate and have him or her find the two types of clauses.

MECHANICS

Use a long **dash** (—) to indicate a break or a pause, or an abrupt change in thought.

Dashes act much like colons, semicolons, or commas, but are less formal, and therefore often appear in advertisements.

> The all-new T595 Daytona signals the dawn of a new era in Triumph's history—technology, looks and performance at the cutting edge of motorcycle design.

> The body work is functional, of course—scything a path through the air to protect the rider, but it's also a masterpiece of style.

1. In your notebook, rewrite the following sentences, adding dashes where appropriate.

   a) This product in case you didn't notice uses the most up-to-date technology available.
   b) Buy Zips and you will have sweet-smelling breath, a charming smile, and most important of all confidence.
   c) If you're in the market for a better spreadsheet program and I know you are this is definitely the one for you.
   d) I'd like to see that movie again maybe next week and I'll bring my friend.

2. Working in groups of three, make up a sentence that might be part of an advertisement for a product. The sentence must have one or more dashes in it. Write your sentence *without* the dashes on a transparency and show it on an overhead projector. Ask each student in your class to write the sentence with the dashes in the right place. Survey the class to see how many students had the correct answer.

3. Find three examples of dashes used in literature that you are reading. Explain their use.

USAGE & STYLE

Language Link

Know
- how a metaphor differs from a simile

A **metaphor** is a figure of speech that makes an implied (or indirect) comparison.

A metaphor, unlike a simile, does not use *like* or *as.* It speaks of one thing as if it were another thing in order to show the connection between the two.

Be Able To
- create metaphors

compares the engine to a cat

The engine <u>purrs.</u>

1. With a partner, discuss why the above comparison is effective. Then brainstorm three other things that the motorcycle could be compared with.

2. Metaphors are a powerful way to make your writing more vivid and original. Create some of your own metaphors by completing the following sentences. (For example, *Her glance was a needle that left a tattoo on my heart.*) Write your metaphors in your notebook.

   a) A fresh orange is a _____ that _____.
   b) The storm is a _____ that _____.
   c) Life is a _____ that _____.
   d) The girl _____ her way through the _____.

3. Collect ads that contain metaphors from magazines and newspapers. With a partner, discuss which metaphors you think work well, and which are less effective. Suggest a different metaphor that might have been used in one of the advertisements.

A Challenge

Eleanor Farjeon uses a series of metaphors to describe poetry in the following poem:

Poetry

What is Poetry? Who knows?
Not the rose, but the scent of the rose;
Not the sky, but the light of the sky;
Not the fly, but the gleam of the fly;
Not the sea, but the sound of the sea;
Not myself, but what makes me
See, hear, and feel something that prose
Cannot: and what it is, who knows?

Marketers often say that to be successful, an ad should "sell the sizzle, not the steak." Write a poem titled "Advertising" that follows the same pattern as Eleanor Farjeon's poem (for example, *Not the motorcycle, but the ...*). What metaphors would you use to describe what advertising does? For ideas, you may want to refer to the ads you collected in activity 3 on the previous page.

Language Link

SPELLING

Know

· common homophones and their meanings

Homophones are words that sound the same, but have different meanings and different spellings. They can lead to spelling problems because it's easy to use the wrong homophone in a sentence.

 Words to Watch For

These words are short and simple, but because they are all homophones, they are easy to misspell. In fact, four of the shortest words below—*to, its, for,* and *buy*—are among the 200 most frequently misspelled words. Most of these words have been taken from the advertisement at the beginning of the unit, while the others are words you will use often.

to	in	you're	weight	for
dawn	way	its	course	buy

In your notebook, make a list of 8-10 homophones. You can use words from this box, the advertisement, and your personal reading.

1. Write a homophone partner for each word in your list. Choose three pairs of words. For each pair, write a sentence that shows the meaning of both homophones (for example, *At the break of dawn I'll don my motorcycle jacket and head out of town*).

Strategy

Sounding out words is not a good strategy to help you spell homophones. Try this strategy instead—create a mnemonic that contains a clue about proper spelling, for example, *The story is a wh<u>ale</u> of a t<u>ale</u>*.

2. Several **Words to Watch For** have more than one homophone partner. In your notebook, write additional homophone partners for these words.

3. **Homographs** are words that are spelled the same but have different origins and meanings. The word *top*, used in the Triumph advertisement, is an example. Look in a dictionary to find the meanings of *top*. Working with a partner, use a dictionary to help you identify three other homographs. Share your findings with the class.

Scroll Back

Edit and proofread your advertisement, paying particular attention to the following checklist:

- ❏ Have you used metaphors and other figures of speech to improve the appeal of your product?
- ❏ Have you used dashes where appropriate?
- ❏ Have you avoided overusing dashes?
- ❏ Are all words spelled correctly, especially homophones?

Present It!

As a class, brainstorm ideas for sharing your advertisements with other students in your school. How about posters, leaflets, or billboards?

Unit 14 **Advertisement**

Unit (15) Review

What is a review?

Reviews are written about all sorts of things: movies, books, CDs, TV shows, computer software, and stage shows. A review provides an overall picture or summary of the item being examined. It also tells people what the writer thinks about the item and why.

Great Canadian Scientists

Publisher: Vr Didatech
Product: CD-ROM
Platform: Mac/Win

Ages: 8 and up
Cost: Approx. $40.00

What do Julia Levy, John Polanyi, and Roger Daley have in common? They're Canadian scientists, and you can find out all about them on this CD-ROM. Packed with activities, games, and video clips, it's designed to highlight the people who make Canada's science scene so great.

Learn why Dr. Birute Galdikas spends half the year in the jungles of Borneo. (Hint: orangutans live there.) Find out what a hypercube is. (No, it's not a cube with way too much energy!) Try out activities and games designed by the featured scientists. For example: play the chromosome game, try to make chemicals react, and use a flashlight to see how red laser light activates anti-cancer drugs. Watch out for a Pop Quiz lurking around the corner! You can find out even more about Great Canadian Scientists and this CD-ROM by checking out the GCS homepage (http://www.science.ca).

At the end of this unit you will

Know

- the characteristics of an effective review
- what a run-on sentence looks like
- when to use italics (underlining) and quotation marks in titles

Be Able To

- write a review
- correct run-on sentences
- use the words *amount* and *number* correctly
- spell words that contain silent consonants

Reviewer
Rosie Amos, Age 13

This CD-ROM is fun and easy to use, but can be a little confusing at times. For instance, the pop quizzes come up randomly, and I didn't get my second chance at any of the questions. I had no problems installing or starting it. I really liked the games and the bright colours and good graphics. I disliked the number of scientists; they said 150 and there were only about ten [looked at in depth] and the games for some of them were not games but projects. I did learn some things: there was a scientist who studied genes and discovered what causes Down's Syndrome. This CD-ROM would be cool on a fast computer with a HUGE screen. Overall, this is a fun educational program.

GREAT
Canadian Scientists
www.science.ca

WRITER'S WORKSHOP

Checkpoint: Review

Discuss how these general characteristics of a review apply to the model. Later, you can use the list to help you revise your own work.

✓ It often begins by describing, summarizing, or providing information about the item being reviewed (e.g., title, publisher, cost).

✓ Aspects of the item the reviewer liked and disliked are then described in detail.

✓ Opinions expressed are usually backed up by examples.

✓ It may end with a recommendation.

1. Choose a book, movie, compact disk, or computer software program that you are interested in reviewing. Consider whether your classmates would be interested in this topic before making your final selection.

2. Make a chart like the one below. As you prepare to write your review, complete each section of the chart. Remember to support your opinions with facts.

Information (title, publisher, cost, plot summary or general description of contents):	
Things I liked and why (facts):	
Things I disliked and why (facts):	
My recommendation:	

3. Write a draft of your review.

4. Read your review to a partner. Ask your partner if he or she has any questions that you did not answer in the review.

5. Revise your review based on your partner's responses and on the information in the Checkpoint. You may need to read, view, or listen again to the item you are reviewing, in order to get more information.

GRAMMAR

> A **run-on sentence** occurs when two independent clauses are joined together without proper punctuation or a connecting word.

I did learn some things, there was a scientist who studied genes and discovered what causes Down's Syndrome.

This CD-ROM can be a little confusing at times, for instance, the pop quizzes come up randomly.

There are various ways of correcting run-on sentences, including

- making two separate sentences
- separating the two clauses by a semicolon
- joining the clauses with a conjunction

1. Explain why each of the above sentences is a run-on, and suggest a way to correct it.

Strategy

To catch run-on sentences in your own writing, read your work aloud. Listen for the places where you pause, and the places where you stop completely. Then check to see that you have put commas or semicolons (pauses) and periods (full stops) in the right places.

2. Correct each of the run-on sentences below, using one of the three methods listed above. Write the answers in your notebook.

   a) This is one of the best movies I have seen the actors are excellent.
   b) The software program features some good ideas, you will only be able to use some of them.
   c) The movie contains some bad acting the characters are not very convincing.
   d) The CD raised my spirits, it made me feel happy again.
   e) This album is definitely her best so far, it contains five outstanding singles.

3. Check your review for run-on sentences and correct any that you find.

Language Link

MECHANICS

Know

- when to use italics (underlining) and quotation marks in titles

Use **italics** or **underlining** for the titles of complete works:

books	magazines	films	newspapers
plays	radio programs	cassettes	computer programs
long poems	TV programs	CDs	

If you are using a word processing program, put the titles of these items in italics; however, if you are handwriting your review, you can underline them instead.

Use **quotation marks** for the titles of items that are part of a longer work:

songs	episodes of radio and television programs
poems	articles in magazines or newspapers
short stories	encyclopedia entries
chapters	

1. Rewrite the following sentences, adding underlining or quotation marks where necessary.

   a) The CD-ROM titled Great Canadian Scientists is a fun educational program.
   b) The Monkey's Paw, a short story, was written by W. W. Jacobs.
   c) Paul McCartney, a former member of the Beatles, wrote the song Yesterday.
   d) The movie Star Wars has become a classic.
   e) I read a review of that CD in The Calgary Herald.
   f) Have you read the book Lost in the Barrens by Farley Mowat?

2. Why is "Great Canadian Scientists" not in italics on page 138 of this unit? Write a rule that explains this usage.

A Challenge

Create a questionnaire to find out students' favourite

- songs
- books
- films
- computer games
- TV shows (or episodes of a particular TV show)

plus any other favourite works you think might be interesting to ask about. Consider how you will present your findings—through a graph, a table, a written summary, an article for the school newspaper, or some other means. Be sure to use italics and quotation marks correctly, both in your presentation and in your questionnaire.

USAGE & STYLE

Be Able To
- use the words *amount* and *number* correctly

Use the word **number** for things that can be counted. Use the word **amount** to describe things that can be weighed or measured, but not counted.

The **number** of scientists covered could have been greater.

The **amount** of information given on each topic was overwhelming.

1. Use *number* or *amount* correctly in the following sentences. Write your answers in your notebook.

   a) There was a tremendous _____ of violence in the movie.
   b) An impressive _____ of reviews were written by our class.
   c) The review indicates that the total _____ of people who tuned in to the television serial on Monday night exceeded 50 million.
   d) Before deciding whether to purchase this program, decide what _____ of time you are willing to spend in learning how to use it.

2. Make up a jingle, rap tune, or poem to help your classmates remember the difference between *number* and *amount*.

SPELLING

Be Able To

- spell words that contain silent consonants

Knock, fright, lamb—it's easy to see what characteristic these words share. Silent consonants can make words difficult to spell because we can't rely on sound to help us. In this unit, you will work with words that contain silent consonants and learn ways that can make spelling them easier.

Words to Watch For

Some of these words have been taken from the review at the beginning of the unit. The others are words you might use when you write your own review. All contain a silent consonant.

scientists	scene	flashlight	technology	column
designed	half	bright	assignment	doubtful

In your notebook, make a list of 8-10 words that contain a silent consonant and that can be difficult to spell. You can use words from this box, the review, and your personal reading.

1. Look at the words in your list. Circle the silent consonant(s) in each word, then look at all the letters that the word contains. Cover the word, picture it in your mind, then write the word.

Strategy

Here are two more tips for learning to spell words containing silent consonants:

- Say the word out loud, including the silent consonant.

- Group your words according to the silent consonant. For each word, say the letters aloud, then write the word.

2. Write the **Words to Watch For** that match these descriptions.

   a) noun; use in a dark room
   b) plural noun; experts in their field
   c) adjective; not usually associated with the night
   d) noun; find this in a newspaper
   e) noun; you may get one of these today

3. Help a partner learn his or her word list. Trade lists. Take turns saying a word to your partner. She or he can spell the word aloud, write it, or draw it using fancy letters.

4. In groups, create a list of at least 20 words with silent letters. In which letter patterns do silent letters seem to occur? Sort the words into categories based on these patterns.

5. Imagine that you have to help someone spell words with silent consonants. What strategies or tips could you give them? (Refer to the work you did for activity 4, above.) Develop three strategies. Give a brief description of each and tell why you think it is effective.

Scroll Back

Edit and proofread your review, paying particular attention to the following checklist:

- ❏ Have you avoided run-on sentences?
- ❏ Have you used italics, underlining, or quotation marks appropriately in titles?
- ❏ Have you used *number* and *amount* correctly?
- ❏ Are all words spelled correctly, especially those that contain silent consonants?

Present It!

Create a "Reviews" wall or bulletin board in your classroom. Every time you read a book, see a film, hear a new tape or CD, or try out a new computer program, post a review for your classmates to read. If two reviews are written on the same topic, place them beside each other so that readers can compare them.

Unit (16) Persuasive Letter

What is a persuasive letter?

Persuasive letters are letters written by a business to possible customers. Their purpose is to convince the recipient to buy a product or service. While business letters such as the one here differ from friendly letters in tone, level of formality, and content, both types of letters require a return address, salutation, body, and closing.

321 Old Chicopee Road
Fredericton, NB
E5Z 8N3

Kildumae
Lawn
Care

*Because your
lawn deserves
a little KLC.*

April 14, 1998

Dear Householder:

My name is Nicholai Kildumae, and I am 13 years old. I am looking for long grass that needs a haircut.

I can do an excellent job of keeping your lawn neat and attractive. I have my own lawn-care equipment (my parents'), including a Honda five-horsepower lawnmower with a mulcher, a gas trimmer, and rakes. I supply the gas!

Last season I cared for five lawns in our neighbourhood. My customers complimented me on being reliable and dependable. One said: "My lawn has never looked so good." All of my customers want me to return this year.

At the end of this unit you will

Know

- the five C's of business writing
- the structure of simple and compound sentences
- the three business-letter formats
- how prefixes and suffixes can change a word's meaning

Be Able To

- write a persuasive letter
- combine simple sentences into compound sentences
- avoid the use of double negatives

My price for cutting an average-sized lawn is $12.00. This price includes mowing and trimming. If you want me to bag the grass trimmings, an additional charge of $2.00 will be necessary. In the fall, if you wish, I will also bag your leaves for a reasonable fee.

My service will operate this year between May 1st and October 15th. I am available for the whole season, special occasions, or just during your holidays.

If you wish to speak to me further, or want to meet with me, please call (555-1234) during the evening. If no one answers, please leave a message on our answering machine. I will call you back as soon as possible. If you prefer, nik@grass.com is my e-mail address.

Yours sincerely,

N. Kildumae

N. Kildumae

Checkpoint: Persuasive Letter

Discuss how these characteristics of a persuasive letter apply to the model. Later, you can use the list to help you revise your own work.

✓ It includes an inside address, salutation, body, complimentary closing, and a signature.

✓ It usually follows the five C's:

Clarity: It explains the services offered and why the company is qualified to provide them.

Completeness: All the information the reader requires to make a decision is included.

Conciseness: It includes *only* the essential information.

Courtesy: A friendly tone gives the reader the impression that the company will act the same way when they are on the job.

Correctness: Mistakes in grammar, mechanics, or spelling might make the reader think that the company doesn't care enough to do a perfect job.

1. As a class, brainstorm a list of possible services you could offer in your neighbourhood (for example, babysitting, shovelling snow).

2. List each of these headings in your notebook, and fill in the information you will include in your letter: PERSONAL INFORMATION, EXPERIENCE, RATE OF PAY EXPECTED, WHEN AVAILABLE, and OTHER INFORMATION.

3. Write a draft of your letter, keeping in mind the 5 C's listed in the Checkpoint.

4. Refer to the Checkpoint and revise your letter until you are satisfied with its focus, content, and organization.

GRAMMAR

Simple sentences contain one independent clause.

> I supply the gas!
> My price for cutting an average-sized lawn is $12.00.

Only one subject and one predicate are found in a simple sentence.

1. Identify the complete subject and the complete predicate in the two sentences above. Then find two other examples of simple sentences in the persuasive letter at the beginning of this unit and identify the complete subjects and predicates in each.

Compound sentences contain two or more independent clauses, joined by a coordinating conjunction *(and, or, but, nor)* or a semicolon.

> My name is Nicholai Kildumae, and I am 13 years old.
>
> My price for cutting an average-sized lawn is $12.00; I will bag the grass clippings for an extra $2.00.

2. Identify the two simple sentences in each compound sentence above.

3. Make the following two simple sentences into a single compound sentence, using a coordinating conjunction.

   a) All our lines are busy. Your call is important to us.
   b) Please leave a message. I will call you back as soon as possible.

Strategy

Combining two simple sentences into one compound sentence is only one way of adding variety to your sentences. You can also

- vary your sentence length,
- include declarative, interrogative, imperative, and exclamatory sentences.

4. The model persuasive letter uses a lot of simple sentences, because they are direct and to the point. Look over your persuasive letter and evaluate your sentences. Have you kept your writing simple, while still including enough variety to make it interesting to read?

Know
- the structure of simple and compound sentences

Be Able To
- combine simple sentences into compound sentences

Independent clauses are covered in Unit 14.

For more on types of sentences, see Unit 10.

Unit **16** Persuasive Letter

MECHANICS

Know

- the three business-letter formats

1. The letter at the beginning of this unit is written in **block format.** Two other formats are **modified block** and **semiblock**. Examine the following diagrams and then summarize the similarities and differences among the three formats.

Block

Dear_____:

Yours truly,

Modified Block

Dear_____:

Yours truly,

Semiblock

Dear_____:

Yours truly,

2. Choose one of the three formats for business letters above to use in your own persuasive letter. Check that you have used the correct punctuation and capitalization as well.

USAGE & STYLE

Do not use negative words like **never, nothing, no**, or **not** after contractions that already contain the negative word **not.**

Be Able To
- avoid the use of double negatives

Double Negative:	I have**n't no** bag on my mower to catch grass clippings.
Correction:	I have no bag.... OR I haven't any bag....

Double Negative:	Nicholai did**n't** receive **nothing** for cutting his own lawn at home.
Correction:	Nicholai didn't receive anything.... OR Nicholai received nothing....

Do not use **not** with the words **barely, scarcely,** and **hardly.**

Double Negative:	He ca**n't barely** get all his lawns cut during the week.
Correction:	He can barely get ....

Double Negative:	I have**n't scarcely** received any calls.
Correction:	I have scarcely received ....

Double Negative:	I could**n't hardly** keep up with the demand for cutting lawns.
Correction:	I could hardly keep up....

I. Rewrite the following passage in your notebook, removing all the double negatives.

I couldn't hardly get up on Saturday morning to get my lawns cut.
I hadn't no sleep the night before. I was so afraid of not waking up,
that I couldn't not get to sleep. I scarcely never have this problem.
I won't barely get my lawns cut today because I'm too tired.
I shouldn't use no excuse for not getting my work done. My
customers won't hardly understand if their lawns aren't cut.

Unit **16** **Persuasive Letter**

Know

- how prefixes and suffixes can change a word's meaning

See Unit 10 for rules about adding suffixes to words that end in the vowels "e" or "y."

A prefix is a word part, such as **un-**, **mis-**, or **im-**, that is added to the beginning of a word. A prefix can change the meaning of a word:

- *cut—uncut* (opposite)
- *dependent—interdependent* (between)
- *similar—dissimilar* (unlike)

Adding a prefix is easy because you don't have to worry about dropping or changing letters. (Adding a suffix, on the other hand, is a little more tricky.)

A suffix can also change the meaning of a word, but in different ways. A suffix can change the part of speech or function of a word:

- *hardness—harden* (a noun to a verb)
- *harden—hard* (a verb to an adjective)
- *hard—hardly* (an adjective to an adverb)

 ### Words to Watch For

These words, most of which have been taken from the letter at the beginning of the unit, might be useful when you write your own persuasive letter. All the words contain a prefix and/or a suffix.

excellent	equipment	reliable	additional	unnecessary
attractive	including	cutting	reasonable	researched

In your notebook, list 8-10 words that have a prefix or a suffix and that can be difficult to spell. You can use words from the box, the letter, and your personal reading. To help you learn the words, underline the prefix or suffix in each word.

1. Circle the root of each word in your list. Choose three of the roots, and for each one write as many related words as you can.

 Strategy

Remembering the shape of a word may help you to spell it. Here is a wordprint for *reliable*.

reliable